HOW DEMOCRATS TURNED ARIZONA BLUE

RIGHTEOUS

AND HOW YOU CAN FLIP YOUR BATTLEGROUND STATE

MIGHT

Matt Grodsky

Righteous Might

How Democrats Turned Arizona Blue and How You Can Flip Your Battleground State

ISBN: 978-0-578-96524-6   Paperback

ISBN: 978-0-578-96525-3   eBook

Photo of Matt Grodsky by Molly McElenney Photography

Book design by StoriesToTellBooks.com

RIGHTEOUS

MIGHT

"No matter how long it may take us to overcome this premeditated invasion the American people in their righteous might will win through to absolute victory."

~President Franklin Delano Roosevelt, December 8, 1941

CONTENTS

To my wife and best friend, Laura Grodsky, thank you for all of your support, selflessness, and patience during this past election.

ACKNOWLEDGEMENTS

This book would not have been made possible without the help of some key individuals.

First and foremost, thank you to my mother-in-law, Ann Scheel, for being the spell-checker-in-chief. She took the time during her demanding schedule to label each section of the book with different color tabs and subsequently made numerous handwritten notes regarding grammar and spelling. I appreciate her time and help on this.

Thank you to one of my many esteemed high school english teachers, Marty Campbell, who introduced me to Biff and Nancy Barnes of Stories To Tell. Biff and Nancy provided invaluable advice throughout the rewriting process and exhibited great patience with getting this published.

Many thanks to the former Arizona Democratic Party Chair Felecia Rotellini for reviewing my work. A huge thank you to my former boss and dear friend, Kelly Paisley, for taking the time to share her key insight in the foreword for this book.

Thank you to my good friend Tommy McKone for all the support during the writing process.

I greatly appreciate all the support from my family throughout this endeavour.

And finally, thank you to the Arizona Democratic Party and their staff. The work you have done and continue to do is a great service to our state and our country.

Matt Grodsky

FOREWORD BY KELLY PAISLEY

Arizona Democratic Party Chief of Staff 2018-2021; Served in the administrations of President Clinton and President Obama, Arizona Governor Napolitano, Senate Majority Leader Mitchell and other top-level elected and appointed officials. State Director for Obama for America and member of numerous White House advance teams.

FLIPPING A BATTLEGROUND STATE, DOING WHAT YOU CAN

When the dust settles after the haboob of an Arizona election cycle, when you have time to assess, heal, reflect, and sleep—many things become clear.

Throughout my career, I have had the privilege of serving in thrilling, diverse roles at various levels of government and political campaigns. Each experience is truly special to me. But, perhaps none more exhilarating as being a part of the team that helped turn Arizona blue for the first time since 1996 in what was arguably one of the most consequential elections in America's history.

Battleground states define elections, they can make or break years of progress. While every Democratic State Party in America is vital, battleground state parties have unique challenges that require unique problem solving. Being the perennial underdog party in a battleground state means that the odds are stacked against you, resources are limited, and your party membership is outnumbered. This was the case for us in

Arizona in the runup to 2020, but while history wasn't necessarily on our side we had something else going for us. We had a great team fueled by hope, grit, and an awareness of our part to play in history.

The simple truth is that no political strategy works without the determined implementation of a state party's staff and it's partners. During the 2020 election, our staff was our family. And that family worked through thick and thin under great leadership to flip our state and contribute to saving our country. Because that's what state parties do, they endure through adversity. We had brilliant team members in each department, dedicated partners on the coordinated campaign and Presidential ticket, and selfless volunteers and community organizers who contributed to the cause. Despite devastating events —a pandemic, the loss of a beloved member of our staff, our building being burned down, and members of our team receiving hateful threats—we prevailed.

Even the most valiant effort doesn't guarantee success in a political race. But we managed to make history in 2020. Arizona's flip to blue at the top of the ticket in 2020 was the culmination of years of hard work by individuals who were committed to making life better for the people of our state, long before we were ever considered a tossup. Amidst the effort of trying to turn the state blue, I often found myself turning blue in the face from holding my breath being unsure of what would happen. But it was all worth it, every painstaking minute.

For those who have been in the trenches, you know that there is nothing sexy about grassroots politics. But every call, door knocked, postcard written, stranger spoken to, makes a difference and the message those individuals receive and who it is received from, is crucial to determining what kind of success your political operation will have. In 30 plus years of service, I have seen messaging that resonated with it's intended audience and messaging that just flat out flopped. Through a strategy of disciplined communications and sound tactics, we succeeded in flipping Arizona in 2020. We sent 11 electoral votes to Joe Biden and Kamala Harris, secured a second Democratic Senator in Congress, retained our U.S. House delegation majority, picked up a Corporation Commission seat, and held our ground in our State Legislature.

There is certainly still more work to be done in Arizona, and we in no way got everything we wanted in 2020. Our state could very easily teater back into the red column and gains made in 2018 and 2020 could be reversed in 2022. But if the party continues to advance the strategies that have led to success in recent years and if more Democrats in other battleground states follow the practices mentioned in this book, then I'm confident that our blue wave can keep rolling across our country for years to come.

For far too long, the radical right has controlled messaging for elections big and small in many right leaning battleground states where Democrats regularly face challenges. This book provides some steps to assist you in combating that unacceptable norm and will help you identify simple and strategic ways to make your message resonate across the political spectrum. I hope that no matter your position with your state party (chairperson, employee, or volunteer) you use the advice offered in the following pages to support your efforts.

In closing, I'm reminded of the story of the hummingbird as told by Professor Wangari Maathai.

> *One day a terrible fire broke out in a forest — a huge woodlands was suddenly engulfed by a raging wild fire. Frightened, all the animals fled their homes and ran out of the forest. As they came to the edge of a stream they stopped to watch the fire and they were feeling very discouraged and powerless. They were all bemoaning the destruction of their homes. Every one of them*

thought there was nothing they could do about the fire, except for one little hummingbird.

This particular hummingbird decided it would do something. It swooped into the stream and picked up a few drops of water and went into the forest and put them on the fire. Then it went back to the stream and did it again, and it kept going back, again and again and again. All the other animals watched in disbelief; some tried to discourage the hummingbird with comments like, "Don't bother, it is too much, you are too little, your wings will burn, your beak is too tiny, it's only a drop, you can't put out this fire."

And as the animals stood around disparaging the little bird's efforts, the bird noticed how hopeless and forlorn they looked. Then one of the animals shouted out and challenged the hummingbird in a mocking voice, "What do you think you are doing?" And the hummingbird, without wasting time or losing a beat, looked back and said, "I am doing what I can."

Like the hummingbird, we did what we could. This book will help you do what you can.

GETTING STARTED

You are a communications professional working at a Democratic State Party in a battleground state. Or perhaps you're on staff at a county party trying to learn how to flip your red state to blue in 2022. Maybe you're thinking about running as a Democrat but want to hone your swing-state message. Or maybe you're just a political junkie trying to figure out winning communications strategies. If you are any of those people, then this is the book for you.

The views expressed here are my own; therefore, this should not be interpreted in any way as an official document representing the views of the Arizona Democratic Party or its affiliate organizations. I use numerous operational examples throughout the book to stress my arguments but have taken great care not to disclose confidential information, therefore any examples and suggestions made should not be interpreted as dissemination of private party information.

By now the results of the 2020 election are well known. Arizona went blue for the first time in nearly a quarter-century. It wasn't an accident or a fluke. It was a deliberate strategy that leveraged 10 years of incremental success to capitalize in the most consequential election in this country's history. While there were down-ballot disappointments, Arizona did not sustain the losses of other battleground states.

This book is about our winning communications model and how our team implemented it in 2020 by executing an effective plan, disciplined politicking in a traditionally conservative state, and rolling with the punches. Today more battleground states are emerging, just as

Arizona was in 2018. I hope to provide a coherent playbook for other Democratic state parties to follow in elections to come.

There has been speculation mania about how and why Arizona voted the way it did, what worked, where Democrats fell short, and what should have been done differently. This book will address that from a communications perspective. It will provide valuable lessons while narratively taking you through our 2020 journey. But I want to be clear that this is not a book about backstabbing, internal drama, or character assassination. If you want dirt, I suggest exploring some of Arizona's splendid hiking trails, there is dirt galore. This is a book from the viewpoint of someone who was in the battle, someone who can explain what the state party did on the communications front to make history happen in Arizona. This book is not a declaration of full credit. I was one cog in a large machine, and our victory in 2020 belongs to everyone involved. So who the hell am I then? Before I dive into the nitty-gritty, here's a quick recap of my background and how I joined this fight.

I have always loved to tell stories. For that reason, my childhood was spent creating movies with my neighborhood friends. When I became a teenager, my passion for storytelling reached a point where I was gaining film festival accolades from around the world, media recognition, and talent representation, and I received a scholarship to attend Columbia College Chicago to study cinema art and science. Throughout my time in college, I frequently traveled to Hollywood to pitch screenplays to managers and producers. The stories I would pitch were political films, often historical adaptations of real events. I even managed to have a couple of screenplays optioned by a production company. But there wasn't a huge appetite in the industry for stories that didn't involve characters in capes.

When I graduated from college, I was engaged to the love of my life, a girl I had fallen in love with when we were in preschool together and whom I had dated all through high school and college. I didn't want to drag her to Los Angeles and turn her world upside down while I tried to make it as a starving screenwriter. So in March of 2016 I began working at a small marketing agency in Scottsdale, Arizona. My job was to lead new business development strategies for digital marketing services. It wasn't my dream job, but it seemed stable, as did the rest of the world. In fact, things seemed like they were shaping up to be better than ever: Hillary Clinton was on course to become the next president, the Cubs were poised to win the World Series for the first time in generations, the Broadway hit *Hamilton* was creatively showing Americans the beauty of inclusivity, everything seemed great.

Despite the fact that it was my company's primary service offering, I was skeptical of the influence that digital marketing and communications had on the masses. That all changed in the wake of November 8, 2016, as I watched Secretary Clinton lose the presidency, due in no small part to Russian interference in the form of deceptive digital advertising, as well as partisan media behemoths that manipulated large swaths of the country through effective communication.

In the aftermath of the ascension of Trump, many people who had never been politically involved suddenly sensed an urgent need to take action. I certainly felt that I had to get in the fight to help stop the damage that would surely come over the next four years and would have far reaching consequences.In the early months of 2017, several things happened almost in tandem that would shape my path to politics. I volunteered on the fledgling gubernatorial campaign of David Garcia, a race that would culminate in November of 2018, assuming David made it through the Arizona Democratic primary.

At that same time, the national press discovered a story about my wife and me that, until then, I had always taken for granted. As I was starting out as a volunteer on the Garcia campaign, Laura and my love story went viral. The digital reach our story had was incredible to watch in real-time. I had to hire a publicist to help me field all the incoming press calls we were receiving as a result of our childhood photos being circulated all over the internet. Our story garnered ongoing coverage from hundreds of media outlets all over the world. Depending on the outlet, articles and interviews have claimed millions of views, likes, and engagements from people across the globe, including celebrities such as Ashton Kutcher, Zooey Deschanel, George Takei, and Tyrese Gibson, who was so touched by our story that he graciously sent us on a second honeymoon through his travel agency. The most touching part of this viral experience was the messages we received from people around the world who were inspired by our love story. Many people sought us out for relationship advice, sent a story about how we had helped their personal love life, or simply shared how they were uplifted by us in the wake of so much apparent bad news.

This experience affirmed three things for me. The first was that good stories resonate and leave a mark on people. The second was that people truly seek hope and want to be uplifted. And the third was that digital media and effective communications strategy could be used for either insidious purposes, as we had seen in the 2016 election, or they could be used to spread profound positivity, such as the story about Laura and me.

November 6, 2018, was the night of the long-awaited midterm elections. Laura and I were in the heart of downtown Phoenix, crammed among a sea of high-top tables and eager Democrats within the halls of the Renaissance Hotel. Before us was a large, empty stage flanked by two giant monitors that showed live CNN election results. Arizona's governorship had just been called for Republican Doug Ducey, less than an hour after polls had officially closed. With a mass groan, a depressed aura crashed down on the room.

This proclamation of victory for Ducey terminated a year-and-a-half-long campaign that Laura and I had volunteered on to elect Garcia for the governorship. He would have been the first Democratic governor elected since Governor Napolitano resigned in 2009 to join the Obama administration. While members of the campaign wept, cursed, and booed around us, I kept my eye on the screens. The race for Arizona's recently vacated Senate seat was neck and neck between Congresswoman Kyrsten Sinema and Congresswoman Martha McSally. I turned to Laura and said, "This isn't going to be decided tonight."

"What do you think will happen?"

I looked back at the screens. Arizona voting results from the 2016 election popped up, a painful reminder of Secretary Clinton's defeat two years earlier. The floating map of Arizona blazed vibrant blood-red on the two screens. I looked back at Laura. "It's going to be close."

As the night wore on, Democrats claimed congressional districts across the state, and we took back the secretary of state's office as well as the superintendent of public instruction post. The night would end with what appeared to be a tight McSally victory over Democrat Kyrsten Sinema. However, within two weeks the numbers had changed, and Kyrsten Sinema became senator-elect with a margin of victory that was just barely 1.2 percentage points. This was the first time Arizona would have a Democratic senator in more than two decades.

A blue wave had swept across the United States in a rebuke to hard-line Republican policies since 2016. As a result, the United States House of Representatives returned to Democratic control for the first time since 2010. I was proud to see the country rise up, despite partisan gerrymandering and voter suppression, and return some semblance of order to DC and state governments across the country. While the victories throughout the nation excited me, I was even more thrilled about the gains Democrats had made in Arizona. Within hours of the election being called for Sinema, the storyline that took shape in the state was that what had once been a Republican stronghold now looked to be a battleground state that could break blue in the next election-2020.

I drove home from the hotel that night reflecting on all the work I had done over the last year and a half as a volunteer. Laura and I had knocked on countless doors, and I had spent money and resources producing content intended to help propel voter interest in Garcia. It was sad to see our candidate lose, but it gave me hope to see us gain control in so many other places. I thought to myself, how can I get more involved? I wanted to be more than a volunteer; I wanted to be on the front lines of the fight as we geared up for the next election. Despite my representation of various government offices, I still felt that I was on the outside looking in. But in 2019 I officially took over as the director of communications for the Arizona Democratic Party and joined a team of hardworking individuals who were committed to making history in 2020.

As the election season drew nearer, it was clear to me that Arizona Democrats needed a new kind of strategy to finally turn Arizona blue and help secure victory. For the longest time we had been underfunded and undermanned in Republican territory. Now we were in a position to win. This is the story about how our communications approach helped turn Arizona blue and the lessons you can take away to flip your battleground state. Let's get started.

I

TO WIN THE WEST

The ramp-up to 2020
and the development of
our communications plan

1

STATE IN PLAY: UNDERSTANDING YOUR COMMUNICATIONS DEPARTMENT

No matter how long it may take us to overcome this pre-meditated invasion, the American people in their righteous might will win through to absolute victory." I couldn't help but think of President Franklin Delano Roosevelt's iconic speech in the aftermath of the attack on Pearl Harbor. Why? Well, it was because I was gazing at a massive portrait of him in my new office. Seriously, this thing was huge and Roosevelt's eyes seemed to follow me no matter where I was in the room. Nevertheless, his *Infamy* speech is one of my all-time favorites, and it was bouncing around in my head all day because of its relevance to where the country was at that moment. His 1941 remarks were a call to action, an assertive rallying cry, and a well executed communications masterpiece that set the tone for the country in the years to come.

On the infamous morning of November 9, 2016, I stoically watched the television as Secretary Clinton conceded the presidency. The election the night before had felt like an attack on the moral fabric of our great nation. We would later learn that it had also been the culmination of a literal attack by a foreign adversary. As Clinton ended her remarks, I wrote myself a note: *Remember this moment. Remember how you feel. Do something so that you never feel this way again.* That declaration had prompted me to volunteer for David Garcia, to navigate my career toward politics, and it had driven me to this moment. Now I was a member of the state party, tasked with helping to lead the charge into 2020.

When I signed on with the party in 2019, it was initially as the digital director, a role that would play a key role in supporting the communications department.In a matter of weeks, I was promoted to acting director of communications based on my previous experience in public relations, and I subsequently took over the role permanently.

Despite all the promise that the post-2018 results offered to Arizona Democrats, nothing was a given and there was no guarantee Democrats would be successful in 2020. Luckily, we had great leadership in the form of our tenacious chairwoman Felecia Rotellini, our no-holds-barred executive director Herschel Fink, and our selfless chief of staff Kelly Paisley. They were all determined to rise to the challenge of turning Arizona blue for the first time in nearly a quarter century and I was eager to help.

Chair Rotellini had been serving as chair for over a year and a half. A former two-time candidate for Arizona attorney general, Felecia had a demanding day job as a high-powered attorney but ran the Arizona Democratic Party in a volunteer capacity. No money and not very much thanks. Nevertheless, she was hell-bent on securing Arizona for the Democrats and often reflected that this was the most important thing she had ever done in her life. I would be working closely with her over the next several months as we shared the party's message with Arizonans and the country.

While there was a heightened level of stress, there was also a great deal of excitement. Not since Bill Clinton's 1996 victory had Arizona gone to a Democratic nominee for president. Before that you had to go all the way back to Harry Truman's 1948 victory, in which he carried every county in Arizona.

The storyline of the state suddenly being in play after two decades of Republican dominance was a new experience for the party veterans. Arizona had a Republican trifecta, meaning the Legislature, the governorship, and the state supreme court were all under the control of the Grand Old Party (GOP). Until the passing of Senator John McCain and the resignation of Senator Jeff Flake, Arizona had been represented by Republican senators and a slew of Republican congressional representatives for decades. Despite there being a slew of long held Democratic congressional seats, majorities had remained elusive. So with the victories of 2018, there was a chance that Arizona could not just go blue but remain so for years.

Part of the logic behind this notion was that, due to the special appointment of Senator McSally to Senator John McCain's seat, the special election for McCain's seat was slated to be held in 2020. Then the regular election for McCain's seat would come up in 2022. And in 2024 Senator Sinema would be up for re-election. Thus, Arizona would be locked in a constant state of political warfare with huge national consequences for years to come. Because of this the state party had to pivot its thinking in 2019 from being longtime lightweights to becoming well-equipped underdogs with the ability to punch up and carry the momentum forward for years to come. No easy task.

The Arizona Democratic Party office was located in downtown Phoenix within an unglamorous yet storied building. The state party split their space with the Maricopa County Democratic Party, which occupied the north side of the structure, and the Arizona Democratic Legislative Campaign Committee (ADLCC), which was infused within the ADP workspace.

The ADLCC was responsible for coordinating messaging and fundraising strategies in support of legislative campaigns in Arizona. The ADLCC, while under the party umbrella, operated independently with their own staff and governing board.Maricopa County and its siblings, 14 counties across the state, also had their own objectives and strategies. The state party was in charge of coordinating with all of these entities with respect to the party's bylaws, the will of the Democratic National Committee, the Democratic Congressional Campaign Committee, the Democratic Senate Campaign Committee, and all of our Democratic elected officials in the state. Each of these entities would soon be working with the coordinated campaign. The coordinated campaign would be the team representing Senate candidate Mark Kelly and would coordinate with the eventual down-ballot federal candidates, as well as any other candidates who could contribute into the coordinated campaign. The goal was to eventually integrate the campaign of the Democratic nominee for president, if the caliber of the coordinated passed the nominee's standards. Ensuring all of our cylinders were firing before teaming up with this colossal operation was vital.

When I took over the communications department I was determined to do whatever I could to help our state party use its messaging might to turn Arizona blue and contribute to the defeat of the most corrupt administration in American history. To help advance that goal, I decided to launch an audit within a couple of days of being on the job. In my previous roles as a marketing executive, I would perform numerous audits or SWOT analysis (Strengths, Weaknesses, Opportunities, Threats)of my clients' operations to find out what could be done to alleviate their pain points. With law enforcement the pain point was almost always quality hiring and retention, with associations it was active membership, and with government agencies it was public relations.

Audits would always yield crucial information that was often over-looked by those too close to the source. They would help develop sound digital marketing and communications strategies intended to achieve the organization's goals. Using a SWOT analysis format, I intended to investigate my new department, given that I was fresh on the scene and could make an objective analysis. The previous communications and digital team from 2018 was a talented group that had helped achieve historic wins. Therefore I really wanted to understand the previous digital and communications strategies so I could gain a comprehensive idea of the framework around our 2018 successes, where we had fallen short, and how we could win in 2020. Communications department heads should strive to understand their department's history and past practices in order to inform future decision making. The next chapter dives into that.

RECAP

+ Democrats felt like we had to strike back from our 2016 loss and get America back on course. Working off of 2018 success, we felt like we were in a strong position for 2020.

+ State parties have to coordinate with various entities under their umbrella, it's important to know what each of these entities are responsible for so that there can be seamless integration with a coordinated campaign in an election year.

+ I joined the team and decided to perform a SWOT analysis of my department.

+ Performing a SWOT can be very beneficial for communications departments to help understand what has worked in the past and what can be improved for the future.

2

TRIAGE: HELPFUL COMMUNICATIONS PROCEDURES

This chapter is dedicated to various practices for communications departments to undertake in state parties. These proved to be essential additions to our communications operations after the conclusion of our SWOT analysis.

Content Calendar: What Are We Saying?

First and foremost, parties must consider the type of content they are producing for their audience. Content should be data-driven and align with messaging on other platforms. All marketing needs to be integrated and consistent. The way I saw it, the party had an opportunity to be more effective by making sure all of our communications tactics worked in tandem. I made it a priority for our executive leadership to have insight into our monthly editorial calendars so they could post from their personal channels in a way that aligned perfectly with our audience-centric messaging goals each month. I felt that social media posts and content should support any press releases the communications department put out versus having these important messaging tools operate in separate vacuums.

I found it helpful to interact frequently with the Democratic Congressional Campaign Committee, the Democratic Senate Campaign Committee, the Democratic National Committee (DNC), the ADLCC, and the numerous communications staffs of elected officials to ensure that nothing fell through the cracks in messaging. Doing this can be time consuming and tiresome, but it is ultimately necessary for communications directors.

We knew we had to engage with the Latinx+Hispanic community. They would be a vital voting bloc in 2020, and it was important that our messaging reached them. I devised a plan to court Latinx+Hispanic media outlets and to issue bilingual versions of our press releases. To this day I recognize that our investment in Latinx+Hispanic messaging needs to be substantially increased, but this plan was a start.

It is vital to track media reach in the form of press releases and interviews. I quickly hired a firm dedicated to tracking media across multiple platforms. It is important for communications teams in a state party to have a real way to measure their media impact. I recommend doing this as it helps communications teams to understand which stories are gaining traction, which outlets are covering you and how often, and what is the general sentiment of the media you are generating.

Democratic parties in other battleground states must identify tools where public relations can be tracked. You need to know how your messaging is playing out, where it is circulating, how people are reacting, and what mediums are performing the best. Political communications cannot be a "pin the tail on the donkey" situation; you need to know what you are doing and where you are going.

At the end of the day, most importantly of all, I knew everyone on our team had to understand who we were speaking to when we engaged with the press, wrote a blog, or made a speech, but just who was our audience?

Who Are We Talking To?

What is a persona? A persona is a composite sketch of a key segment of a marketing audience. Anytime an organization wants to drive someone's actions, they need personas to help understand what messaging and mediums will be most relevant and useful to their audience as a whole.

In my experience, parties have limited time and resources, so developing personas using this three pronged approach is advisable::

1. Leveraging Google and Facebook transparency reports, you can see who similar organizations are targeting for their advertising initiatives. This helps you see how various advertising campaigns are performing based on strong audience segments. It gives you a sense of how to set expectations and target audiences that would perform well for you. (Even as Facebook and other platforms change their targeting abilities, there will still be ways to identify key attributes that will allow you to engage your ideal audience.)

2. Once you are able to establish audience tracking on your website and advertising platforms, you can use the data to help shape who your personas actually are. Where do they live? How old are they? What demographic are they from? What is their economic background? What matters to them? You then marry the data with polling and to help verify your persona information.

3. Comb through your email subscribers (this is likely nearly a hundred thousand names) to help identify which personas are donating the most money in state and out of state. This data can be used to determine future ad targeting efforts.

If you can't afford major research firms, these tactics are crucial. When defining personas it can feel like there are infinite possibilities. As a rule of thumb, I always suggest creating no more than five personas that home in on where you see opportunity. It's not meant to explore every feasible audience type. So this is where we started.

The following voter personas are not the ones that were created to help the party's targeting strategy but they should give you an idea of what persona information entails. I want to stress that it's okay to refine personas over time, we certainly did. Our personas were not perfect by any means, and there were still a fair amount of assumptions in shaping each identity; still, this brought us closer than ever before to understanding who we were speaking to, who we wanted to interact with more, and how our words might impact those who were not in our targeted audience:

STRONG-SCHOOLS SALLY

+ 34-year-old, work-from-home, suburban mom with two young children.

+ Sally is worried about the quality of education her children are getting in their public schools. She also sympathizes with teachers who are being underpaid and thinks that the state needs to do more to help them. She supported Red for Ed.

+ Sally and her husband worry about the economy and the cost of healthcare, especially considering their aging parents in Santa Cruz County.

+ Sally voted for David Garcia in the last election.

+ Sally is considering giving some of her time to help the Democrats in 2020 but is not sure how; the idea of knocking on doors is nerve-wracking.

+ Sally lives in northeast Phoenix.

HEALTHCARE - HEADACHE HAROLD

+ 55 years old. He is upper middle class with higher education.

+ He worries about the rising cost of healthcare and job security for his adult children in Arizona, who all have student debt.

+ Harold voted for McCain in 2008 and Romney in 2012. These days he identifies with centrist Democrats.

+ Harold lives in Scottsdale, with his wife and two dogs. Harold hopes to retire within seven years from his job as COO of a company that relies on international trade and a healthy local economy to be successful.

JOB-JUGGLING JUAN

+ Juan is in his early twenties. He recently graduated from a community college and is considering a higher degree. He speaks English and Spanish.

+ Juan works two jobs.

+ Neither job offers healthcare, which is concerning for Juan as he will be off his mom's insurance in two years.

+ Juan was raised Catholic and drives from his apartment every Sunday to attend church with his family as long as work doesn't get in the way.

+ He begrudgingly voted for Hillary in 2016 even though many of his friends did not. He thinks DACA (Deferred Action for Childhood Arrival) recipients should be able to become citizens but immigration is not his biggest concern.

+ Juan really wants better job security and better education without being crushed by debt. He would like to be able to buy a home and have nice items. Having a strong economy with plenty of work is key to Juan. He doesn't consider himself to be very political and doesn't obsess over political news, although he does understand the broad appeal of patriotism and family values expressed within GOP messaging.

+ Juan lives in Tucson.

ALWAYS-ABANDONED AVA

+ 28 years old. Lives in Apache County.

+ Ava has started to become more engaged politically.

+ Ava is anxious about the economy. The unemployment rate in most Native American communities in Arizona is over 20%.

+ Land deals and voter suppression are major concerns for Ava.

+ Ava is frustrated that no one seems to be listening to her community's concerns.

If You Do Nothing Else, Please Track

State party digital or communications teams must maintain and protect their website. Key maintenance practices include making sure that your site is properly set up for Search Engine Optimization (SEO). If it isn't then you run the risk of your site missing out on relevant traffic because key search terms you should be found for are not identified in your site. This can damage search rankings and your messaging exposure.

Battleground state parties should develop three objectives for your advertising campaigns based on what you know will motivate your persona audiences. Despite the platform being heavily saturated with ad campaigns throughout Democratic primaries, I suggest substantially leveraging Facebook as an advertising source. My three suggested objectives for advertising are:

1. Raise money: inspire donations

2. Promote the brand: explain Democratic values

3. Drive Voter Action: volunteer, register to vote, go vote

Assumptions are Cancer

The most important thing for other battleground state party communications leaders to remember when it comes to advertising and marketing is that assumptions you have about your party brand are not facts about your brand. That's just you talking at a group of people, hoping they will see things your way. Whether the goal is to raise money or get someone to vote, understanding your audience's perception of your brand and their pain points needs to be what drives your political advertising and marketing, no matter what action you want your persona to take.

On the video front, have a robust editing platform with content specifically curated for social media platforms. As of this writing, I like Promo or Canva for quick and easy videos. Final Cut ProX or Adobe should be considered if you want to go one notch up. Yes, these are investments but they will allow your team to quickly and fairly easily generate content that is specifically curated for social media platforms for a reasonable cost. It would allow us to create high-quality videos for ads and social channels at an effective volume. I also asked that we invest in Canva Pro, a graphic design platform that allowed us to edit images for various mediums. We needed these tools so we could be aggressive with our content. Other state parties seeking cost-effective platforms to help generate content in an efficient, user-friendly manner should consider tools such as these.

Ultimately, the SWOT analysis did more than just help my department; it allowed my team to work better with the other departments in our office. Knowing crucial things about our personas would help other elements of our staff achieve their objectives and, hopefully, secure our victory in 2020.

RECAP

+ Make sure your party representatives are speaking with one voice and that you are looping them in on the messaging objectives

+ Engage and coordinate frequently with party partners to ensure cohesion.

+ Please measure and track your media. This will help you gauge how your message is performing and where you get the most reach

+ Develop audience personas so you know who you are speaking to.

+ Advertise with messaging that is inspired by your persona data.

+ Track your audience data on your website and advertising platforms.

+ Make cost-effective investments in tools that will help your team with content creation that speaks to your audience.

3

BATTLE PLAN: SHAPING A SWING STATE COMMUNICATIONS STRATEGY

Vince Lombardi was a Midwest Democrat and a brilliant football coach. I say that not as a biased Packers fan but as an admirer of strong leadership. It depends on who you ask and which website you're willing to believe, but one of the most compelling phrases believed to have been coined by Lombardi is "Hope is not a strategy." That phrase was flashing in my mind as I concluded my audit and flew to Wisconsin for an annual family gathering in July of 2019. As Laura and I observed the 4th of July parade in Whitefish Bay, I began putting the pieces together in my mind.

As far as communications were concerned, my plan was to implement a winning strategy based not on hope but on data. This chapter seeks to better explain how we identified our audience personas, which in turn helped drive our strategy.

Arizona's 15 Counties

As I enjoyed my time in the Midwest, I could not help but think of Secretary Clinton's missed opportunities in the Rust Belt.

A Map of Arizona's 15 Counties

In the closing days of the 2016 election, Clinton made a pivot to the Sun Belt, specifically, Arizona. At the time, there was speculation that the state might be in play. With hardly any investment late in the game, Clinton managed to get within striking distance of Trump on election night. She lost the state by roughly 4.5 percentage points.

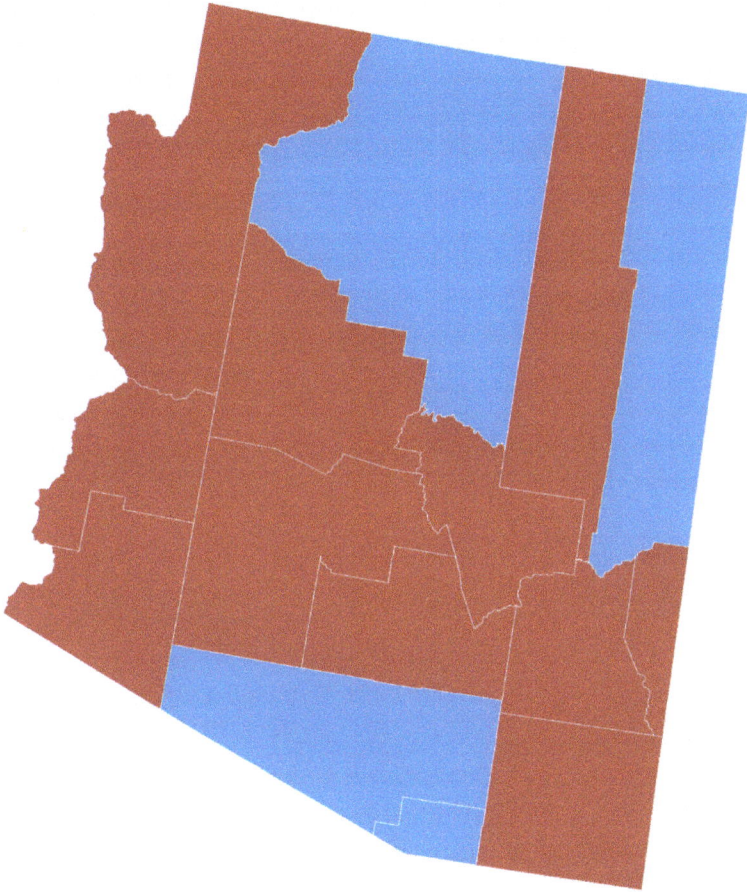

2016 Election Night Results for the Presidential Race (Blue Counties went to Clinton, Red Counties to Trump) Politico magazine

While her strategy would later be scrutinized and picked apart, there was a silver lining for us in the Grand Canyon State. Her close loss signaled to Arizona Democrats that the state was winnable. This is what led to our victories in 2018 and would form a basis for our ongoing communications tactics throughout 2019 and into 2020.In the

2018 midterms, David Garcia, who ran as a progressive, lost the gubernatorial race to incumbent Doug Ducey. However, Blue Dog Democrat Kyrsten Sinema won the Senate seat against Republican Martha McSally and carried the ever crucial Maricopa County, which Garcia lost handily:

2018 Won Counties Percentage of Vote to Garcia:

- Santa Cruz: 62.5%
- Apache: 59.7%
- Coconino: 55.9%
- Pima: 50.2%

2018 Lost Counties Percentage of Vote to Garcia:

- Mohave: 19.0%
- La Paz: 22%
- Graham: 24.2%
- Gila: 27.4%
- Yavapai: 29.7%
- Cochise: 32.1%
- Greenlee: 32.6%
- Pinal: 33%
- Navajo: 37.3%
- **Maricopa: 42%**
- Yuma: 43%

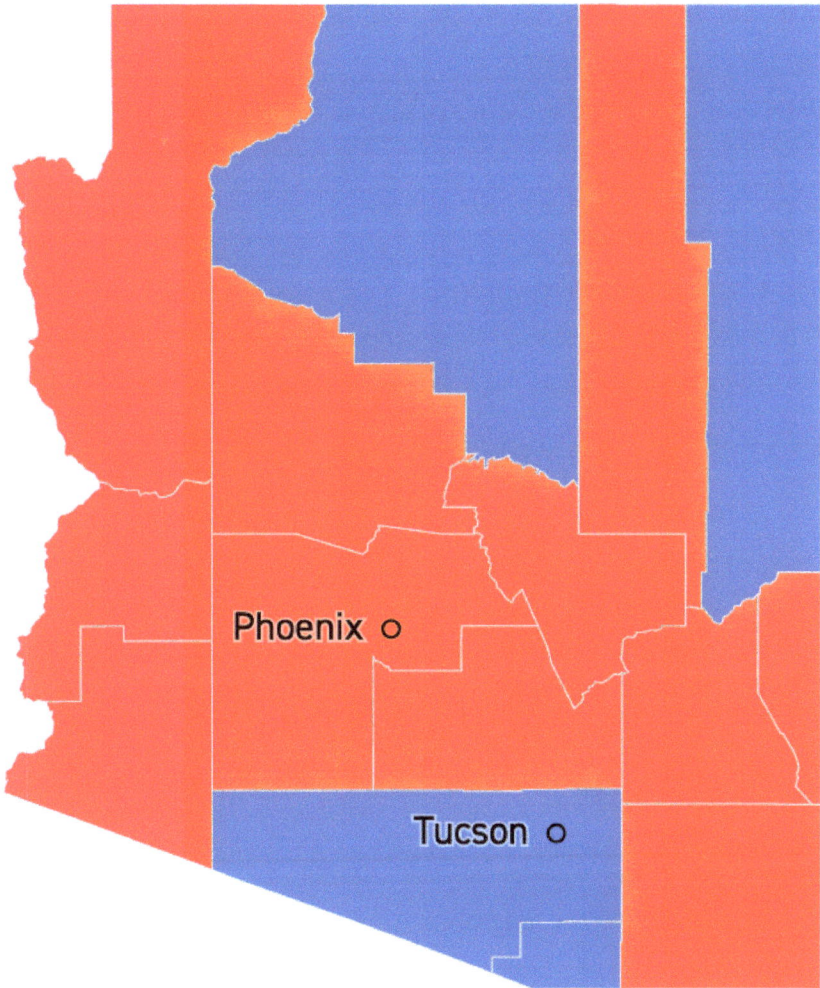

2018 Election Night Gubernatorial Race Map Results (Blue Counties went to Garcia, Red Counties to Ducey) Politico magazine

Compare those results to the same night's results for candidate Kyrsten Sinema in the Senate race.

2018 Won Counties Percentage of Vote to Sinema:

- Santa Cruz: 58.5%

- Apache: 65%

- Coconino: 62%

- Pima: 56.7%

- **Maricopa: 51%**

2018 Lost Counties Percentage of Vote to Sinema:

- Mohave: 26.9%

- La Paz: 31.7%

- Graham: 31.8%

- Yavapai: 37.1%

- Gila: 37.3%

- Cochise: 38.2%

- Greenlee: 40.6%

- Pinal: 42.9%

- Yuma: 45.4%

- Navajo: 45.4%

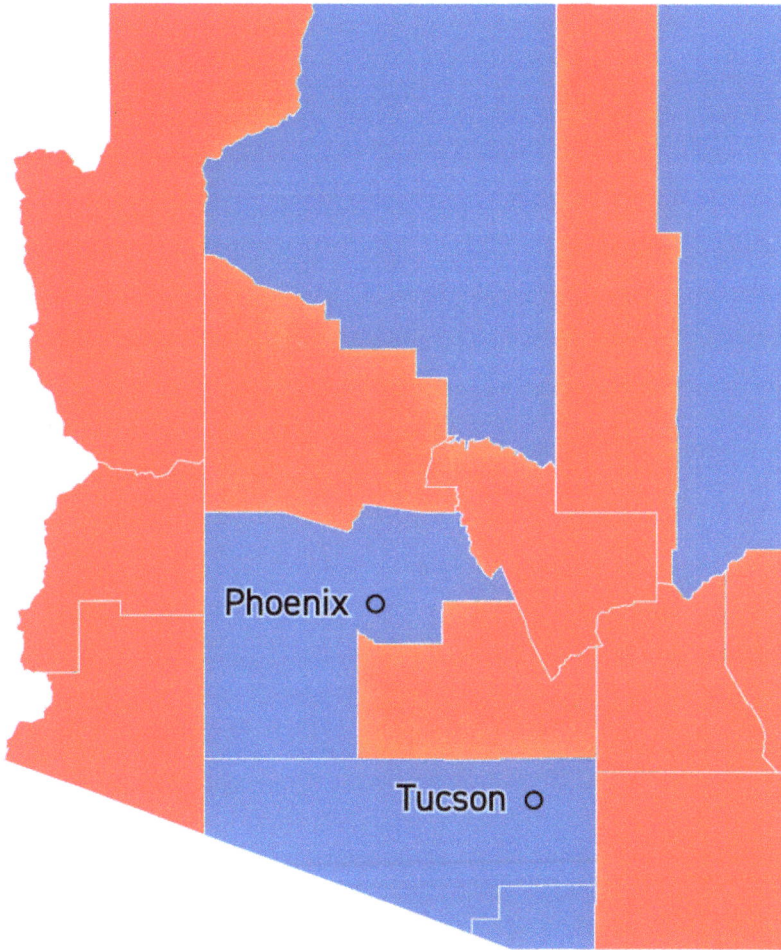

2018 Senate Race Map Results (Blue counties went to Sinema, Red Counties to McSally) Politico Magazine

Sinema's victory was narrow: roughly 38,000 votes, or 1.7 percentage points. But she beat McSally and claimed Jeff Flake's seat in the Senate. Sinema was able to carry Arizona's most populous county, Maricopa County, which has save for trivial fluke incidents always decided state-wide elections. She carried Maricopa County with over 50% of the vote.

Garcia only carried 42% of Maricopa county and lost it. Statewide, Garcia lost by roughly 15 points.

Sinema and Garcia ran on different playbooks for statewide office. Sinema's campaign recognized that Republicans outnumbered Democrats in the state and that there were as many Independents as Republicans. She worked to persuade voters in the center, knowing that the Democratic Party would be loyal to her even if she struck a centrist tone. Garcia, in contrast, made a bold appeal to the progressive base in an effort to awaken the sleeping liberal giant and drive an energized electorate to the polls. Pundits had already taken note of this difference in strategy and later analyzed how it had ensured one candidate prevailed while the other was trounced.

Understanding the reasons why Garcia lost and Sinema won would become a key part of our long-term strategy. But another aspect we were trying to understand was which counties had higher turnout. We were able to identify that the counties with some of the highest turnout and vote percentage that favored Democrats also had some of the highest donation rates to our state party, a key indicator for enthusiasm.

Red bars indicate counties that set records for turnout

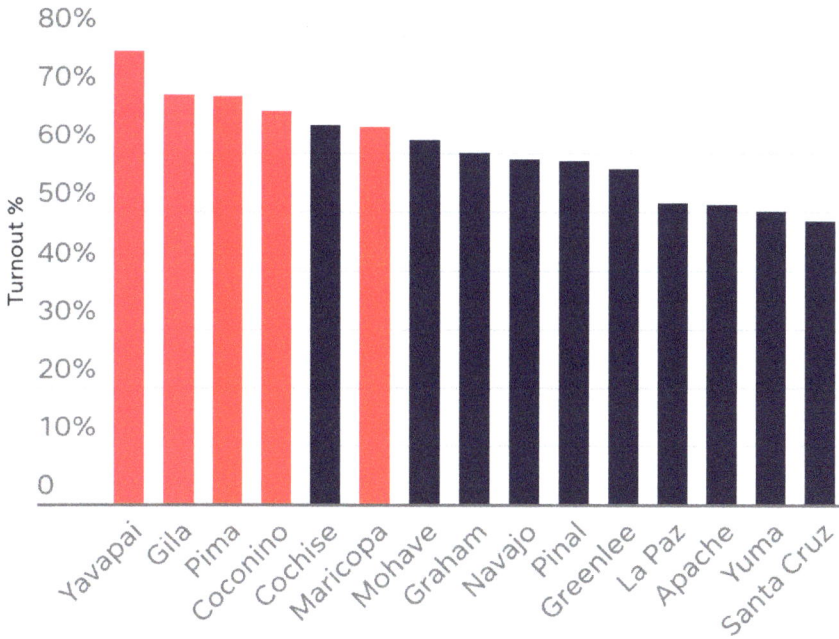

Source: Latest estimates and historical data from Secretary of State's Office
Graphic by Agnel Philip

2018 Arizona Turn Out Results by County, The Arizona Republic, www.azcentral.com

We were able to use all this various information to cross-check individual donors with our email lists, past interaction with our digital advertisements, and their past voting history. This allowed our audience to take shape in our minds.

As I pored over the data, it also revealed interesting information in the counties Democrats won versus the counties they lost. It has been observed in various battleground states that Democrats do better with younger voters. I recognized this quickly in counties across Arizona. The same could be said for communities where there were higher rates of minorities, and more women than men. Generally, more-educated communities favored Democrats in 2018. How should you read demographic data on your state's counties?

Here is a snapshot of county demographics in the aftermath of the 2018 election:

- Santa Cruz: 83.4% Hispanic, 15% white; Median age is 36, Gender Ratio: 92 men to 100 women.

- Apache: 72.8% Native American, 18.5% white; Median age is 34, Gender Ratio: 98 men to 100 women.

- Coconino: 54.3% white; 25.8% Native American, 13.9% Hispanic, Median age is 30, Gender Ratio: 97 men to 100 women.

- Pima: 52.6% white, 36.6% Hispanic, 3.2% black; Median age is 38,Gender Ratio: 97 men to 100 women.

- Maricopa: 56.3% white, 30.6% Hispanic, 5.1% black, Median age is 36, Gender Ratio: 98 men to 100 women.

It was surmisable that Democrats did worse in counties that were whiter with a median age of over 50 with more men than women with less education. For example:

- Mohave: 78% white, 15.9% Hispanic, Median age is 50, Gender Ratio: 101 men to 100 women.

- La Paz: 58.7% white, 26.3% Hispanic; 11% Native American, Median age is 56, Gender Ratio: 105 men to 100 women.

- Graham: 51.2% white, 32.5% Hispanic, 12.6%; Native American, Median age is 33, Gender Ratio: 115 men to 100 women.

- Yavapai: 80.9 % white, 14.3% Hispanic, Median age is 52, Gender Ratio: 96 men to 100 women.

- Gila: 62.8% white, 18.6% Hispanic, 15.6% Native American, Median age is 50, Gender Ratio: 99 men to 100 women.

- Cochise: 55.7% white, 35% Hispanic, Median age is 40, Gender Ratio: 103 men to 100 women.

- Greenlee: 47.6% white, 46.4% Hispanic, Median age is 33, Gender Ratio: 110 men to 100 women.

- Pinal: 57.4% white, 29.6% Hispanic, Median age is 38, Gender Ratio: 109 Men to 100 women.

- Yuma: 62% Hispanic, 31.8% white, Median age is 34, Gender Ratio: 105 men to 100 women.

- Navajo: 43.2% Native American, 41.6% white, 11% Hispanic, Median age is 35, Gender Ratio: 101 men to 100 women.

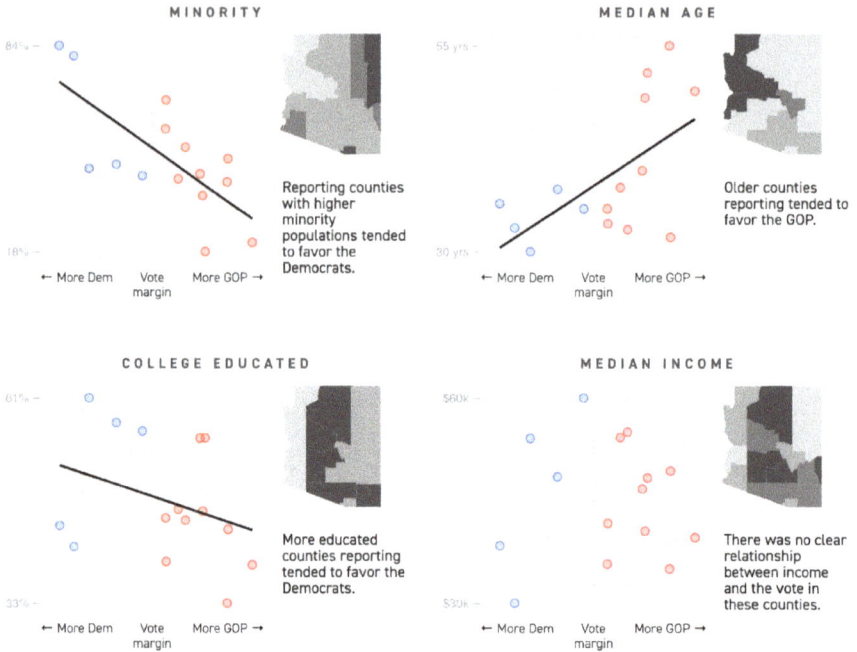

AZ County Demographics Breakdowns from Election Night 2018 Politico magazine

Having this understanding of county demographics allowed us to give an identity to our voters. It helped to explain why turnout was better in certain pockets of counties and helped us to frame what motivated a certain person to vote for Democrats. We cross-checked our website traffic audience and social media audience against these findings. We found that they matched up with the type of voters who were coming out for us in elections and were even located in the same geographic regions where we performed better

Website Rush Hour

Measuring website traffic is a must-do in order to square your targeted audience with who is actually showing up on your site and why.

The majority of site traffic came from Phoenix, Tucson, and Tempe. This was consistent with our county data.

- 27% of azdem.org visitors were 25 to 34 years old; this correlated with the voting blocks we did best in by county.

- 21% of users were 65+.

- 54.3% of users were male.

- 45.7% were female.

The Wilderness of Twitter

I find Twitter to be the Wild West of politics, oftentimes, a cesspool of animosity and a buffet of endless clap-backs. Regardless, it's the chosen medium for the political times we live in, and therefore, a necessary evil. ADP's Twitter account had some 20,000 followers when I joined the party. Twitter's audience was vital to understanding what engaged some of our most fervent supporters.

- Primary Audience: Men/Women 18 to 34

- Best posting times: 10 am to 12 pm; 2 pm to 4 pm; 6 pm to 8 pm;

- The 18 to 34 range correlated with our county data. The higher female percentages were also consistent with our county data.

- 20,000 followers.

The Facebook Machine

Audience insight is a crucial component of Facebook. Speaking to some 30,000 followers, we needed to know what messaging worked and what didn't. Tracking our audience allowed us to analyze our users and identify unique interests we didn't know existed.

- Primary Audience: Women 65+.

- The top locations: Phoenix, Tucson, and Tempe.

- Best Posting Times: Morning/Midday/Early Afternoon. Fridays had the most page traffic.

- 30,000 followers.

The Gram

Facebook's sexier cousin, Instagram, had a younger and less prevalent audience. The account had been created fairly recently and had the most ground to cover in terms of social media platforms leveraged by the party.

- 31% of users are 25 to 34 years old, followed by 35 to 44 at 22%, 45 to 54 at 13%, 55 to 64 at 9%, 65+ at 6%, and 13-17 at 2%.

- Top locations: Phoenix, Tucson, and Tempe.

- 56% were female versus 44% male.

- Best days to post: Thursday, Friday, Sunday, Monday.

- Best times to post: 9 am to 9 pm. The largest spike was 6 pm.

- Women 25-34 years old were the most active on our page.

- 1,400 followers.

What are They Thinking?

Now that we knew where our voters and donors were, we could see how they were engaging with the party. But we still needed to understand their mindsets. According to multiple 2018 exit polls and ongoing data, we were able to learn a lot of crucial information that would help us prepare for 2020.

Healthcare and education were the biggest issues for Democrats. In one notable exit poll from 2018, 42% of Arizona respondents said healthcare was the main issue, and 77% of those voted for Sinema. Democrats clearly performed better in urban environments with more diverse audiences that skewed younger—below 40 years old—and had higher levels of education. For instance, roughly 60% of people in urban environments broke for Sinema in 2018, with roughly 39% going for McSally. Notably, some 54% of people in the suburbs went for McSally versus Sinema who had 44%. The ages 18 to 44 went for Sinema by roughly 59%. We were able to hone in on these numbers, and through the painstaking work of investigating additional metrics collected after the election, we were able to get a clear picture of what was motivating voters from both parties.

Mission Latinx+Hispanic

In the run-up to 2020, we were incredibly aware thatLatinx+Hispanic voters were now north of 30% of Arizona's population. The expectation was that this demographic was a dormant volcano that would erupt in favor of Democrats any day. I have observed a frequent misconception over the years that immigration is the key issue motivating Latinx+Hispanice voters group.The fact was (and arguably remains) that economics and job creation were among the top issues for these voters and were the key to effective communication. Demographics for any group are not identical in each battleground state (Arizona's Latinx+Hispanic voters vs. Florida's for example) but getting past assumptions and leveraging real data, especially when it comes to minority populations, is vital for your messaging success.

Data we obtained after the 2018 midterms showed us that roughly 42% of Hispanics aged 18 to 34 voted Democrat, 49% identified as Democrats, 28% were undecided. Also, 32% of Hispanic millennials were undecided, and some 40% of all Hispanic respondents indicated a motivating factor to vote would be, *"If I felt my vote would make a difference."* Notably, some 22% of Hispanics and 30% of non-Hispanics supported Donald Trump's policies and liked his leadership style.

Who is Voting?

For the longest time I had heard that, *"Republicans outnumbered registered Democrats by 140,000+ and that there were as many Independents as Republicans."* I worked with our voter file manager to collect the necessary information from the various recorders across the state to identify which counties had voter registration deficits or surplus. What we found was compelling and provided a visual image we had previously lacked.I recommend this for other battleground states.

It should come as no surprise that almost every county that went red in 2018 had more registered Republicans than Democrats. The path to victory was in these numbers. We had to close the gap in essential

County	Democrats	Republicans	Party Greens	Libertarians	Other	Total People	Dems vs Reps
Apache	28,356	9,141	48	151	12,390	50,086	19,215
Cochise	19,074	28,087	114	539	23,806	71,620	-9,013
Coconino	34,295	21,443	281	800	27,081	83,900	12,852
Gila	8,656	13,155	27	177	7,993	30,008	-4,499
Graham	5,181	8,504	12	87	4,449	18,233	-3,323
Greenlee	1,840	1,439	3	36	1,278	4,596	401
La Paz	2,294	4,196	13	39	3,755	10,297	-1,902
Maricopa	679,243	807,404	3,602	21,899	774,187	2,286,335	-128,161
Mohave	19,815	56,718	132	695	41,611	118,971	-36,903
Navajo	24,805	21,643	84	392	17,228	64,152	3,162
Pima	214,540	165,708	1,445	4,563	171,123	557,379	48,832
Pinal	54,793	73,381	295	1,574	74,679	204,722	-18,588
Santa Cruz	14,288	4,667	48	148	9,295	28,446	9,621
Yavapai	29,384	66,905	268	1,063	45,382	143,002	-37,521
Yuma	30,595	26,152	69	585	32,704	90,105	4,443
Total People	1,167,159	1,308,543	6,441	32,748	1,246,961	3,761,852	-141,384

July 2019 Arizona Counties Registration Numbers Maricopa County Recorder's Office

counties, Maricopa being the primary target; otherwise, top-of-the-ballot races would be at risk and down-ballot races would be in critical danger.

Personas are Born

Now that we had unpacked the data, it was time to truly define our "voter personas." This idea came from my experience in marketing land. Whether it was on behalf of our own agency or our numerous clients, we would always develop "personas." The purpose was to be able to recognize and articulate a certain type of consumer for a specific business in order to cater messaging to that persona so that it would drive a specific action. Politics was no different. With our data in hand, we went about fully fleshing out Strong-Schools Sally, Job-Juggling Jose, Healthcare-Headache Harold, Progressive-Planet Patty, and Always-Abandoned Ava.

RECAP

+ Hope is not a strategy, and too many operatives and parties rely on it to usher in victory.

+ State parties must understand and define their state's personas.

+ Audience insights from our website, ad platforms, and email lists, married with county information and polling data, helped us discover who our voters were.

+ You must know what messaging will resonate with each of your personas. It is imperative that you ensure that your methods of reaching these audiences are working.

+ State parties must know their election and voter history and know specifics about their state's voter registration numbers.

4

PERSUASION: TALKING TO A BROAD AUDIENCE

"Choose wisely, Democrats. If we lose Arizona, we could lose the White House." That was the title of Fred DuVal's op-ed in The Arizona Republic on July 31, 2019. DuVal is an Arizona civic leader, member of the Board of Regents, a former Democratic gubernatorial candidate, and former senior White House staff member. DuVal's piece alluded to the successful election victories of center-left strategies executed by Bruce Babbitt, Dennis DeConcini, Janet Napolitano, and most recently, Kyrsten Sinema. He posed the hypothesis that centrist Democrats could win in Arizona because they had a track record of doing so, and given the importance Arizona would play in 2020, it would be unwise to deviate from that strategy.

"While it's tempting to fall in love with candidates who meet every aspirational ideal, this year we must apply a different—more pragmatic—standard. Progressive Democrats make a different case that a more ideologically pure candidate will ignite record turnout of new voters that will make the difference on election night. This was the theory of David Garcia's courageous campaign for governor last year [2018]. He and Sinema were both good candidates with much to offer, but the electoral difference between them was a significant 15 points."

I agreed with DuVal's assessment. The data I had poured over backed it up too. The Arizona GOP had made a strategy to tie itself to the Trump brand, despite the president consistently losing favor among the majority of Arizonans. Many of us understood that the state was purple with the potential to go blue should the stars align in 2020. We would need to commit to energizing our base voters while persuading on-the-fence Arizonans and moderates who were wary of Democrats but turned off by Republicans. There was in fact a large swath of John McCain moderates who held true to traditional Republican ideals—low taxes, small government, a strong military—but were appalled by Trump. Many of those McCain Republicans were either switching party affiliation or at least casting their vote for candidates like Sinema. I understood this was an audience we had to continue to nurture and attract.

At the same time, it was vital that we not alienate our progressive base. This would all require a thoughtful approach, one where we could thread the needle and pull off a victory by going to bat on key issues but striking a tone that was free of much of the fiery rhetoric that could pass in bluer states. We had to have a Goldilocks mentality: not too hot, not too cold, just right. The same approach must be considered for Democrats in other battleground states. Promote your values and don't alienate your constituents, but follow a thoughtful playbook to bring others into your tent. It isn't easy but it is imperative in battleground states where the margins are tight and every vote is crucial to success.

Now that we had our communications tone settled, how would we get our message across?

Chair Wars

Aside from the party platforms, nothing contrasted the Arizona Democratic Party and the Arizona Republican Party more than the personalities of their respective chairs. The Democrats were led by Felecia Rotellini, an attorney, former prosecutor in the Arizona Attorney General's Office who served as Superintendent of the Arizona Department of Financial Institutions under Governor Janet Napolitano and ran for Attorney General in 2010 and 2014. Chair Rotellini was ever insistent on the need to elect leaders with integrity who would set a good example for the constituents they represented. Rotellini had gained immense respect among Democrats within all sectors of the party as well as moderate Republicans who appreciated her pragmatic approach.

Arizona Republicans were led by the infamous Kelli Ward, a former state representative and a two-time candidate for Senate. Chair Ward gained notoriety among Republicans and Democrats for her far-right views and her Sarah Palinesque ability to say the darndest things. Ward was endeared to President Trump, and despite polling that suggested Trump's approval was underwater in Arizona, Ward was all in on the Trump mantra.

As 2019 began to wind down, I felt it was important to provide an opportunity for Arizonans to witness the two state party chairs discuss their positions in an interview.Strategically, I knew Felecia would come off as much more relatable and well-intentioned than Ward, who traditionally appeared bombastic. Brahm Resnik of NBC's local affiliate, 12 News and host of *Sunday Square Off*, a local version of *Meet the Press*, agreed to host the unprecedented event in a live interview that would take the entirety of the 30-minute program.

Due to great preparation, the segment was a success. Rotellini came off as calm, authentic, and above the fray of politics. "Let's make integrity great again." was her most notable quote. She discussed health-care protections, defending Medicare and Social Security, and the fact that Arizonans wanted leaders who would put them first. Ward, on the other hand, picked fights with Resnik, defended Trump's actions in Ukraine, belittled the Democratic Party, and sought to make the case that Democrats were scheming to ruin Arizona. If a voter were to have tuned into politics for the first time, and had been hoping to gain a sense of the difference between the two state parties, this interview pro-vided a golden opportunity for us to entice that voter or at least show them that our side was operating in reality.

If you have a state party chair that is comfortable doing press and the circumstances make sense for a square off with the chair of the other party, it presents an ideal opportunity to contrast each party's values and integrity.

Rural Counties Count

Like many battleground states, there were many rural counties throughout Arizona that were deep red. However, some of our pro-gressive strongholds existed in Southern and Northern Arizona's rural areas. Despite Maricopa County, the most populated county that included the state's capital, being the ultimate decider for the upcoming election, it was imperative that we maintained our strength in our rural blue zones. But there was an electorate expansion opportunity as well.

For example, there were many lifelong Republicans located in Nogales, Arizona. Nogales is a thriving port-of-entry city on the U.S./Mexico border in Santa Cruz County. Billions of dollars flow through Nogales every year. The city's economic strength is reliant on trade and visitors from Mexico. With the asinine trade policies of the Trump administration, there were many Reagan Republicans in Nogales who were switching parties or were considering doing so. Those folks were our opportunity.

Over the course of several months, our chair and key members of our senior leadership would do a series of high-profile tours across rural counties with the specific goal of nurturing Democrats but also bringing independents and former moderate Republicans into the fold. We attended the Navajo Nation annual parade, toured deep-red districts, and participated in forums that included Republican lawmakers and audiences. Many Republicans we interacted with had varying reasons for their "born again" mentality. Some of it was trade, for others it was the deficit. Many took issue with Republican attacks on pre-existing-condition healthcare coverage, and several felt that the GOP had been consumed by an immoral blackhole since Trump's ascendancy. We maneuvered to harness that discontent and plug these Republican refugees into the Democratic Party.

There were even deeper-red Republicans we branched out to. At a Democratic debate watch party in July of 2019, I spoke with a young Trump supporter who was in attendance. Everyone was apprehensive of this person but I approached him. He was a big hockey fan, a Grand Canyon University student, loved beer, and was skeptical of global warming, especially given that he was from the freezing cold Dakotas and came from a community that was reliant on oil and gas jobs. After speaking with him about Republicans I admired, and connecting over hockey and beer, I realized he was genuinely curious about the Democratic Party. Fox News had painted a picture for him that we were a socialist party looking to overtax, steal guns, and let immigrants invade the country. I politely explained what Democrats actually stood for and that we understood the issues that were important to him. I tried to explain what global warming was, and he was receptive.I didn't convert this young man to the party in our brief conversation, but I know he left the event with a new view of Democrats. We felt it was important to listen to skeptical voters who may not have always agreed with us, especially if they were interested in learning about us now. We took that mindset into the rural counties we visited. No one was off limits if they expressed an interest in engaging with us. This is an important lesson for communications folks in other battlegrounds, no one who engages with the party in good faith should be off limits.

Supporting County Parties and Legislative Districts

A quick note on county and legislative district messaging; every state is different but I would suggest providing as much communications guidance and support to county and legislative district party teams as possible. These organizations are typically run by volunteers with a lot of heart and limited resources. While messaging points may vary from region to region, it is helpful to counties and legislative districts to have guidance and frequent help from the state party communications team. Sometimes counties and legislative districts will have their own messaging priorities and that is okay. The point is to be in contact and provide support, it helps to ensure the state party and counties are on the same messaging page. A good way to do this is to share your content calendar with them and provide weekly, if not daily, talking points.

Courting the Private Sector

Republicans had cornered the market on being the party of business and sound economic policy. This was despite Republican administrations consistently dragging the U.S. into recessions and giving enormous tax breaks to corporations, which ultimately weakened the economy. Nevertheless, many Arizonans carried the perception that Democrats were the party of social issues but Republicans knew the business world. We were committed to changing that view.

In the final two quarters of 2019, we rolled out our Copper State Business Advisory Board. It was a forum made up of 60+ CEOs and business owners who were seeking direct, conversational access to elected Democrats and party leadership. Our argument was that Democrats were poised to make huge gains in the state Legislature and even expand our congressional delegation in Washington, so if business leaders in Arizona wanted a seat at the table in the new regime, they had better start talking to us now. We set up quarterly gatherings that would cover key economic issues facing the state. Business leaders would get an opportunity to share insight and ideas with Democratic leadership, essentially laying the groundwork for action if Democrats ultimately took control of the state legislature.

This type of healthy engagement builds relationships, creates messaging ambassadors, and combats the incorrect notion that Republicans have a patent on sound economic policy.

Engaging Republican Refugees

We worked to amplify the discomfort of moderate Republicans, since they were the most influential people with moderates in Arizona. Several key Republicans made a point of voicing their opposition to the direction of Arizona's current Republican party. Without overdoing it or looking crass, we shared and communicated some of these statements through our channels and made an effort to put them in front of moderates and independents.

"I can see [Arizona] going Democrat, I really can," said Cindy McCain, John McCain's widow, during an interview for *Politico*'s Women Rule podcast. "I'm not saying I want that, but I can see it happening." She went on to say that there were two major reasons why: one has to do with changes in the state, and the other stems from the transformation of the Republican Party during the presidency of Donald Trump. "We have a huge Hispanic population now that have found their voice in politics, number one. And number two, we have on my side of the aisle—on the Republican side—we see a local party in Arizona that's not functioning well, and it's excluding people," said McCain. "If you're not walking the line, then you're out. That's just not right. That's not the party that my husband and I belonged to."

Grant Woods, who was a Republican when he was elected Arizona's attorney general in the 1990s but who converted to a Democrat in 2018, publicly stated that, "There is not much Republican left in the Republican Party."

In the fall of 2019, the Arizona Democratic Party also hired an Emmy winning director, Harry Gantz, to develop two digital videos to be used for Facebook advertising. One video would highlight Arizona Democratic voters and be advertised to like-minded Democrats across Facebook. The other video would highlight recently converted Republicans who became Democrats. The video would be targeted at independents and moderates in Arizona in an effort to bring them over to the Democratic Party.

Finally, we would follow a strategy of **ABCs**. In sales this translates to Always Be Closing. In this case, I personally wanted to translate this as **Always Be Campaigning**. The way I saw it, we were a brand that was a flagship for dozens of candidates. We needed to be messaging 24/7 until all the results were in on Election Night 2020.

RECAP

- We made a cohesive effort to clarify the differences between Republicans and Democrats at the state level. Oftentimes, bubbles can form around people who work in the same field every day, and it can be easy to forget that what looks obvious to them may not look so obvious to the general public. Explaining clearly, without condescension, the difference between the two parties proved essential.

- It was vital that we follow a Goldilocks type of playbook that relied on the middleground. Battleground states like Arizona need to follow this kind of path to build coalitions.

- We put the entire state in play by touring every county instead of just emphasizing Maricopa County.

- We amplified the sentiments of moderate and former Republicans who had become disenchanted with the direction of their party.

- Anyone across the political spectrum who engages with your message in good faith should be given the time of day.

- Communicate regularly with county and legislative district parties, provide communications support and information so that they stay on message and have a reliable partner.

- Engage with business leaders and integrate the party with private sector relationships. Corporate leaders and private organizations can help amplify your message and this can help break down the misconception that the GOP is the "economy" party.

5

SELF SABOTAGE AND SPACESHIPS: HANDLING COMMUNICATIONS HICCUPS

Communication strategy is a dance. Your communications team requires careful movement and discipline. When your plans are effectively executed, risks are mitigated and messaging is productive. But there are always inevitable bumps in the road that will test the mettle of your team. Some of those bumps occurred before the final bell of 2019.

In September of 2019, the Arizona Democratic Party was gearing up for its final state committee meeting of the year. For those who don't know, these gatherings are an opportunity for members of the state party to come together to vote on important policies that can be adopted into the state party's platform and structure. This has implications for a variety of things, from supporting massive policy initiatives to making sure that venues we rent for events adhere to our party values. The state committee is made up of various committees and caucuses and culminates in one large plenary session where resolutions are voted on in accordance with Robert's Rules. These things can last for hours and hours … and hours.

Can't We All Just Get Along?

Before I get down in the weeds on this, let me be crystal clear. The Democratic Party has a spectrum of left, right, and center. Each state party in this country has that same spectrum on a micro-level. We are a big tent party, one very large family that can argue and piss each other off, but at the end of the day, we are just that—family. To reiterate, this section is a reflection of my personal observations and opinions, not the party's.

The Arizona Democratic Party state committee is made up of precinct committee members from across Arizona, roughly some 800+ people. In one interview I described state committee meetings as "a big Thanksgiving dinner" with differences of opinions expressed within what is ultimately one big, happy family. There was an extra tinge of drama on this particular meeting since the progressive caucus, the left wing of the state party, had issued a public resolution for consideration that called on Senator Sinema to be censured for not aligning herself with the tenets of the party. Regardless of who was right or wrong in this situation, this was arguably not the type of story we needed in the runup to the election.

A censure is effectively just a figurative slap on the wrist. It holds no real consequence other than being embarrassing for the state party and the senator. Needless to say, this resolution had the potential to create a bad media narrative on the eve of an election year. Sure enough, as soon as news of the censure became public, local and national media swarmed.

Despite how ill-conceived the resolution was from a strategic point of view, in a year when Democrats had an opportunity to flip the state blue, I could not throw the progressive caucus under the bus in the press. Why? They represented a significant group of the state party and were a bastion of our Democratic values. I framed the matter to the press in the following terms so that we could take some of the air out of the idea that the censure was predetermined to pass and that it was in fact symbolic. I told them this was a resolution that would have to pass through a resolutions committee, facing possible amendments, before it could even be considered by the full party, where, even there, it could potentially be struck down.

I also explained that the whole point of state committee meetings was for all factions of the party to express their views. And the chair and I reiterated that the Arizona Democratic Party was thrilled to have Senator Sinema representing Arizona in the Senate.

Convoluting my message, however, were expressive members of the progressive caucus who took it upon themselves to talk on the record with the press about their grievances with Senator Sinema. It was certainly their right but was just not helpful in the broader scheme of trying to help candidates win across the state under the Democratic brand.

The Arizona Republic reported at the time: The state coordinator for Progressive Democrats of America, told *The Arizona Republic* the censure is intended to encourage Sinema to move back toward the left, where her political career began.

"Here's the thing: We really support Kyrsten Sinema, we want her to succeed, we want her to be the best senator in the country. But the way she is voting is really disappointing. We want Democrats to vote like Democrats and not Republicans." Felecia Rotellini, Arizona Democratic Party chairwoman, said the censure will be heard and discussed. She is uncertain if it will pass. "We are a very diverse group and that means diversity of thought, as well," Rotellini said. "I don't think it reflects poorly on the party at all, I don't think it's an indication of a fracture. I think it's an indication of a group of people who think differently and have a different perspective on the same topic."

Luckily, when the state committee meeting occurred, the resolutions committee unanimously recommended tabling the notion of formally censuring Sinema. Co-chairs of the party's resolution committee said during their huddle that the progressive caucus opted to delay any action to censure Sinema until January 2020.

I was relieved to see this happen, but I knew this would certainly rear its head again the following January. While I understood and personally sympathized with many of the feelings motivating the censure, and while I even in 2021 share many of those same frustrations, I felt at the time that we had to mitigate any sign of disunity as we approached 2020. Communications teams in other battleground states will undoubtedly face similar challenges when dealing with the inner workings of state parties.

Teaming Up

With Arizona finally being in play, the DNC in 2018 and again in 2020 issued a coordinated campaign to come in and assist the state party. That campaign was called Mission for Arizona (M4AZ), a play-off of Mark Kelly's experience as an astronaut.

Coordinated campaigns, whether they be in Democratic stronghold states or in battlegrounds, are made up of highly skilled team members with varying backgrounds in politics, many of them from out of state.

The coordinated campaign was a team that worked in tandem with the Mark Kelly campaign for senate and the Democratic presidential nominee. The chair spent significant time helping to brand and integrate the coordinated team into ours. Mission for Arizona consisted of staff members who often specialized in the same areas as members of the state party. In my case, I had multiple counterparts on the communications front. Mission for Arizona was funded by partner campaigns and individual donors. Generally, the top of the ticket provides the majority of the campaign's resources and funds a statewide program that benefits all candidates on the ballot—hence the term "coordinated." Mission for Arizona's primary goals were:

1. Winning the U.S. Senate seat for Mark Kelly.

2. Sending Arizona's 11 electoral votes to the Democratic presidential nominee.

3. Winning competitive U.S. House races.

4. Gaining Democratic seats in the state Legislature.

Mission for Arizona would officially launch on February 18, 2020. But the ramp-up was happening in 2019. M4AZ was tasked with handling much of the tactical ground-game elements of the 2020 cycle and would help spearhead a powerful Get Out The Vote (GOTV) program. They would rely heavily on the support of the Arizona Democratic Party, which would help facilitate communication to the county parties and legislative districts. The timeline for the coordinated campaign encompassed four phases with varying objectives:

Phase 1: September 1st — April 2nd:

Right out of the gate, the volunteer base would need to be activated. Mission for Arizona would identify supporters and volunteers from previous cycles and re-activate them so that the party had a deep volunteer apparatus.

Phase 2: April 3rd — August 6th:

This phase would be all about shaping the electorate and priming it for action. The program would start registering targeted voters, signing them up for the Permanent Early Voting List (PEVL), and committing voters to cast their ballot for Democrats.

Phase 3: August 7th — October 1st:

Phase three would focus on scaling the organization. M4AZ would prepare the tactical teams for election training that allowed them to run a GOTV effort across the state.

Phase 4: October 2nd — November 3rd:

Once ballots were sent out, M4AZ would run down supporters with ballots and educate them to ensure a higher ballot return rate. After the 30, M4AZ would chase supporters still with ballots and make sure they put their ballots in the mail or were able to vote. The program would focus its efforts on increasing turnout among supporters who were traditionally, for whatever reason, less likely to turnout.

For Immediate Release

Tuesday, February 18, 2020

Contact: press@missionforarizona.com

"Mission For Arizona:" Arizona Democrats Launch Statewide Coordinated Campaign To Elect Mark Kelly And Democrats At Every Level Of The Ballot In 2020

The coordinated campaign will launch with several senior staff in place and a dozen organizers on the ground, with first two offices opening this week

PHOENIX — Today, Arizona Democrats are launching "**Mission for Arizona,**" a unified statewide campaign to elect Mark Kelly and Democrats up and down the ballot in 2020, as well as lay the groundwork to deliver Arizona's 11 electoral votes to the eventual presidential nominee.

The coordinated campaign will launch with several key senior staff already in place, and with over a dozen dedicated organizing staff already on the ground, as well as Latinx outreach and voter protection staff.

Today's launch marks the earliest that Democrats have ever launched a statewide coordinated campaign in Arizona. Building upon Democrats' 2018 successes, Mission for Arizona is on pace to be Arizona's largest and most ambitious coordinated campaign ever.

Mission for Arizona will serve as Democrats' central hub for resources, organizing, and political infrastructure in 2020. The coordinated campaign will focus on electing Mark Kelly, winning competitive U.S. House races, flipping Arizona's state legislature, and delivering Arizona's 11 electoral votes to the Democratic presidential nominee.

"We're thrilled to launch this statewide mission to build on our historic success in 2018 and elect leaders who will take on corporate interests, put people first, and fight to make Washington and the state legislature work for Arizonans," **said Emma Brown, Mission for Arizona's Coordinated Campaign Director**. "This is a critical election, and we're going to harness the unprecedented energy we're already seeing on the ground in Arizona to pull off another year of big wins."

Mission for Arizona is launching with two initial field offices opening this week in Phoenix and Tucson. The campaign plans to open another office in South Phoenix within the next month, with more offices across the state to follow. Additionally, the campaign is launching a digital hub to leverage heightened volunteer and voter engagement online.

✦ ✦ ✦

The linkage between the state party and a coordinated campaign presented great promise but also challenges that often required ironing out early. In our case, both groups sought Democratic victory in 2020. But one was working on behalf of specific candidates at the federal level while the other was serving as a brand ambassador for the party's values, its down-ballot races from school board to state Legislature, 800+ members of its state committee, Democratic National Committee brand, and the state's currently elected Democrats.

Coordinated campaigns and state parties can easily develop different objectives in day-to-day operations, based on the different stakeholders each group represents.We were fortunate to work out the kinks and identify clear areas of responsibility. I would meet regularly with their communications team to ensure cohesion. Ultimately, the coordinated campaign oversaw our field-organizing initiatives in order to enhance our ability to register voters, get people signed up for the Permanent Early Voting List, and mobilize action across the state. They were an invaluable part of our efforts.

Shit Happens

Murphy's Law states, "Anything that can go wrong will go wrong."That's true. I had signed our chair up to take part in a panel hosted by KJZZ and Clean Elections called "We the Voters". The panel included the chairs of the state's major parties: Republican, Democrat, Libertarian, and Green. It was a softball opportunity on a Saturday in October 2019 to talk about the party's values. The event was being recorded by the Clean Elections team.

Now, for context about what was going on at the time, the Trump administration had recently and foolishly announced a withdrawal of troops from Syria, effectively abandoning our Kurdish allies, who would now fall prey to ISIS militants and Turkish troops. Just as Trump was abandoning those forces, he committed nearly 3,000 troops to Saudi Arabia, arguably not the most historically reliable U.S. partner for a series of reasons, which further complicated an already fraught geopolitical situation and sparked a bipartisan backlash.

At that time Saudi Arabia was in the spotlight for an additional reason. The crown prince's apparent involvement in the assassination of journalist Jamal Khashoggi, to which Trump had been lambasted for essentially shrugging off the issue and not holding the prince to account despite international outrage. So amidst those daunting and complex current events, the Clean Elections panel was underway on that sleepy Saturday with a handful of spectators who had shown up to hear the party chairs speak.

Speaking broadly about electing leaders who put people first, and then attempting to contrast Trump's plethora of failings, Felecia stated, "Another reason why people are going to vote (is) because Donald Trump is manipulating the White House and has aligned himself with ISIS and Saudi Arabia." Ward immediately jumped on the ISIS comment and tried to spin it as a slanderous literal accusation by claiming that it was not true. I'm certain she was eagerly trying to wrap this in with the "Russia witch hunt" narrative that the right wing was focused on perpetuating at the time. Amidst Ward talking over her, Felecia tried to drive home the importance of electing leaders who don't enable America's foreign adversaries.

The event quickly moved on from there and covered a range of topics. Felecia's remark, reasonable when considered in the full context of current events, would not have been a big deal if it weren't for the fact that, within hours of the comment, the Trump administration announced that a military operation at the president's instruction had killed the leader of ISIS.

I had a horrible feeling that between the unfortunate timing and the possibility of the GOP editing together a hit piece, the press was going to get on us for this. But in hopes of not drawing unnecessary attention to the mishap, we decided not to engage on the comment until someone tried to level an attack.

But sure enough, it was like a bomb exploded. As soon as Clean Elections released the video of the event, the AZGOP jumped at it and cut up a video of Felecia's comment, contrasting it with the death of the terrorist at Trump's behest and attempting to frame it as though Felecia's comment had been a slanderous, literal accusation. The local and national press leaped at the story, and the right wing, with the help of Ward, fueled it for days. I issued a clarification in the press, articulating that the word choice was poor but that the comment was in reference to Trump's reckless foreign policy, which experts across the government had already made clear.

The Arizona Republic reported: "It was a poor choice of words," Matt Grodsky, spokesman for the Arizona Democratic Party, said in an email to *The Arizona Republic* on Tuesday.Grodsky said the comments stemmed from, "President Trump's haphazard decision to withdraw troops from Syria, which has been opposed by Republicans and Democrats alike because it abandoned our Kurdish allies in the fight against ISIS, empowered Iran, Russia, and the Syrian regime, and hurt our interests in the region."

Once I put that statement in the universe, it cauterized the wound, and soon the press pivoted from "what was that thing she said" to "well, what she was trying to say was." The coverage died down a few days after we clarified, but what lasted for much longer were the hideous messages left on our office's answering machines and sent to our emails. The messages were a melee of angry right-wingers expressing their outrage at speaking so ill of their dear leader. It was the death threat over the phone, leveled against Felecia, which forced us to alert the police.

In hindsight I should have issued a statement immediately after the event, effectively blunting the story before it could metastasize. We could never have known that on the same day as the event, ISIS was about to be a major headline with the death of its leader. But after the raid I should have put us out in front of the pending circus. Had we clarified right out of the gate, we could have softened the blow. What's important is that we recovered and learned. Another item worth noting is the importance for communications directors to set some guidelines before events of this nature. If I had a time machine, I would have gone back to negotiate a more focused list of topics for the panel instead of the wide ranging, free wheeling event that it was. Especially with an opponent like Ward in the mix, structure like what we had in the Sunday Square off showdown was vital. The takeaway here is that communications teams do not have to capitulate to the structure of every media opportunity and it is incumbent on them to make sure that the media opportunity is structured to be as beneficial to their cause as possible.

RECAP

- In a large apparatus like a state party, you won't always be able to control the public opinions of everyone involved. It is important to develop contingencies and strategies to cope with events beyond your control and find a way to mitigate risk.

- Coordinated campaigns require collaboration early on and throughout the cycle of an election year. Constant communication and establishing clear objectives is key to a healthy relationship.

- When in doubt, get out in front of a bad statement; it will save you hours of headaches later.

- Mistakes in the press are bound to happen. Don't compound the mistakes by making more of them through inaction.

- You have a say in how events with the media are structured, especially when they involve an official from your party or a candidate you're assisting.

6

IMPEACHMENT: COMMUNICATING AN ISSUE WITH AN EYE TOWARDS POLLING

I n the final months of 2019, Owens Harkey Predictive Insights, under the leadership of Mike Noble, released new polling that showed Trump's approval rating was sinking in Arizona, a loss of five points between May 2019 and August 2019. The majority of Arizonans disapproved of his job performance. In the Senate race, Mark Kelly maintained a narrow lead over McSally. On issues once thought to be kryptonite for Arizona Democrats, there was beginning to be wiggle room. For instance, independents were swinging in favor of tighter gun restrictions in the wake of the mass shootings in El Paso and Dayton. In the fall election, Propositions 105 and 106, which conservative dark-money groups were pushing in order to kneecap Phoenix's budget and derail the public transit system, were overwhelmingly defeated by voters.

The political situation in the state was starting to look like Blockbuster Video. For decades the movie rental industry had enjoyed a monopoly in their market until the blitz of streaming services like Netflix, Hulu, and Amazon. Within a few years, Blockbuster was in a fight for its life to stave off aggressive competition that had never before been a factor. We all know how Blockbuster ended up. But this competitive market was how it was shaping up for Republicans in Arizona. Their hold on the electorate was eroding at a rapid pace and Democrats were increasing our share. In an interview around this time, Noble stated, "The national implication for Arizona is at a zenith [...] If you would have said four or five years ago that the Democrats could have two U.S. senators, people would be looking at sending you to the looney bin."

Inquiry after inquiry from the media was in regards to the Democrats' momentum and how we would use it in 2020. One of my statements to the press regarding our promising position read, "After a long string of broken promises from Donald Trump and Arizona Republicans, Arizonans are ready to make a change in 2020. We are feeling confident about the year ahead amidst a strong fundraising year and with an increasingly energized electorate. Over the course of the next year, Democrats will continue to highlight the issues that are most important to Arizonans, making the case that we're the party that will make Washington and the state Legislature start working for every Arizonan, not just the powerful special interests and the wealthy few."

All in all, we looked poised to head into 2020 with the wind at our backs. Then came news of a now-infamous call between President Trump and Ukraine President Zelensky.

The Crook in the White House

As a brief recap, Trump abused his power and pressured Ukraine to help his reelection campaign by announcing investigations into a then-potential 2020 opponent, Joe Biden. OnJuly 25, 2019, in a call with President Zelensky, Trump asked Ukraine to "do us a favor" and investigate a conspiracy theory about the 2016 election and Joe Biden, dangling much needed—and Congressionally approved—military aid as the incentive for Ukraine to capitulate. In other words, Trump had established a quid pro quo. Under the leadership of Speaker Pelosi, the House initiated a months-long impeachment inquiry to uncover the facts.

Knowing this would be a sensitive issue in our state, I had the party issue a statement that did not mention impeachment directly but voiced support for Democrats pursuing the facts in order to uphold the rule of law. Even though many of us, including myself, believed the president deserved to be impeached, we needed to ensure we did not overplay our hand.

For Immediate Release

September 25, 2019

Arizona Democratic Party on U.S. House Impeachment Inquiry

In response to House Speaker Nancy Pelosi announcing the House will proceed with an official impeachment inquiry, Arizona Democratic Party Chair Felecia Rotellini released the following statement:

"The Arizona Democratic Party has full confidence in the leadership of Speaker Pelosi and her judgment to do the right thing.

"As a co-equal branch of Government, Congress has the right to investigate this Administration for any wrongdoing. President Trump must cooperate. No one is above the law. Arizonans deserve to know if the President of the United States risked our national security to gain dirt on a political opponent and engaged in a gross abuse of power.

"We must take action and get all of the facts. If the administration does not cooperate with Congress on the investigation, then further action will be required."

✦ ✦ ✦

As the House investigations pressed on, more information came to light that was damning for Trump. Ambassador Sondland, who "followed the president's orders," told Ukraine the military aid they had been promised would not be released, and Ukraine would not get the White House meeting they sought until they announced the investigations Trump wanted. Former Ambassador Bill Taylor told investigators that Trump made the release of military aid contingent upon Ukraine announcing those investigations.

The facts were clear. Trump put his personal political interests over America's national interest by soliciting foreign interference in the 2020 election and withholding military aid to Ukraine. Trump then obstructed Congress. He refused to comply with the congressional investigation and blocked members of his administration from testifying, despite lawful subpoenas compelling them to do so.

At Trump's direction, 12 aides refused to testify in the inquiry. Congress made 71 specific requests or demands for documents. Not a single one was turned over. Past presidents who were subject to an impeachment inquiry complied with legal demands for documents that Trump refused.

Give the People What They Want

Our team kept a careful eye on polling data in Arizona. In an op-ed by Mike Noble published in *The Hill* that December, he stated, "Polling in November showed that Trump's job approval is underwater by 4 points (46 percent/50 percent). Both Trump's job approval and the impeachment question break down almost evenly on party lines. Among independent voters, Trump's job approval is -13 points. But independents also oppose impeachment by 7 points. The data indicate that Democrats may have jumped the shark on impeachment power with Arizona's all-important independent voters."

Despite the polling, Arizona's U.S. House Democrats voted in favor of impeachment. It was a moral question of historic proportions: make a political calculation or stand up for the Constitution? As a party, we had to walk the fine line of commending the elected officials who did the right thing, without pouring too much gasoline on the issue and alienating moderates in our state.

A piece by Shadi Hamid in *The Atlantic* magazine summed up the political dilemma this way. "Every Democratic politician is asking—Is impeachment at this moment a good idea politically, and [...] is it a good idea for the country? To do nothing would be to shrug their shoulders in the face of one of the most corrupt presidents in modern history [...] Democrats had to do something. The president has been wrong and done wrong, and his misdeeds must be recorded somehow. There is something to be said for upholding basic constitutional principles, irrespective of outcome, especially when future scenarios can comfortably remain in the realm of the imagined. Or more fatalistically[...] Maybe sometimes you gotta do something even if it's a bad idea. Democrats have probably made the right choice. It's just a choice Americans may have to pay for."

On December 18, 2019, the House of Representatives took the historic step to impeach President Trump, charging a president with high crimes and misdemeanors for just the third time in American history. The House voted almost entirely along party lines for two articles of impeachment to remove the president from office: abuse of power and obstruction of Congress. As the two articles of impeachment cleared the House and moved onto the Senate, all eyes were on Senator Sinema.

We knew that if she voted against impeachment, she would gain more praise from moderate Republicans but further infuriate the progressive base of the Democratic party just in time for another state committee meeting where a censure vote would certainly carry new momentum in January of 2020. Another issue brewing around us was animosity from the far right towards Democrats' decision to defend the Constitution.

Crazy Season Comes Early

My wife and I were in New York City on vacation. We try to do a trip every December around the date of our wedding anniversary. On the morning of December 19, I got a message from Kelly, our chief of staff. The Arizona Democratic Party headquarters had been tagged on multiple sides of the building. Crimson spray paint in menacing letters read, "SHAME."

We assumed this was retaliation for the impeachment vote. Not believing anyone would take credit online, but still fervent about covering our bases, I scoured social media for signs of someone gloating or for any threats stated on our channels. Meanwhile, our office filed a police report. My search yielded little results. Among the normal grumbling of conservative trolls, there were some messages from questionable accounts that demanded Democrats leave Arizona and take our crazy ideas with us. Some of the accounts had violent usernames, which gave me cause for concern. I passed them on to our executive team and suggested we include them in our report to law enforcement.

Many members of the staff were rattled by the office vandalism, several employees fearing that this was the first of many things to come, likely with escalation. Ironically, I was fielding all of this information outside the memorial of the World Trade Center. Viewing the solemn pools that traced the footprints of the twin towers, I thought back to the days in 2001 when Americans became united in the wake of tragedy. It was a stark contrast to the division we faced now. Standing at the site of the memorial, I also remembered brave souls that day who refused to be deterred by acts of terrorism.

While a simple act of vandalism registered as absolutely nothing in comparison to that colossal tragedy, the eerie discomfort our employees felt was real. For some members of our staff, the memory of the assassination attempt on Congresswoman Giffords eight years earlier that had claimed the lives of some of their friends and wounded others was still fresh. The fear was that vandalism of the building, inevitably covered by the media, would inspire a more-hostile actor to escalate harassment on our staff. In the aftermath of our chairwoman receiving death threats, hate mail arriving in our inboxes, right-wing fanatics boasting of taking political matters into their own hands by using their guns, and amidst a country drowning in daily mass shootings, the concerns were valid and would, unfortunately, be validated in the months to come.

Despite these genuine fears, I made the point to senior leaders of the party that this action was designed to scare us, that we could not be seen as cowing to acts of intimidation. I stressed the importance of issuing a defiant statement, not intending to be provocative but to show that we would not be bullied. As the press appeared, looking for our reaction, we released a statement from our executive director: *"We're proud of our Democratic House members for standing up for the Constitution, and we're not ashamed to be fighting for better wages, lower prescription drug costs, and affordable healthcare for every Arizonan."* It was important that we appeared unfazed, that we stood by our convictions but also pivoted back to the issues that truly mattered to voters, the issues that would determine the outcome of the next election.

As we raced towards New Year's Eve, it was clear that impeachment in the Grand Canyon State was still not as popular as it was in some other parts of the country. An OH Predictive Insights poll showed 47% of Arizona voters were opposed to impeachment and removal, with 42% in support. According to Data Orbital, an Arizona-based GOP consulting firm, the majority of Arizona voters in a poll on impeachment opposed removing Trump from office; 52% of respondents opposed convicting Trump of impeachment and removing him from office. Only 43% said they supported removing him.

We had to take polls with a grain of salt, but it was important to leverage data. Would the impeachment issue finally push Trump's approval rating above the 50% mark in Arizona? Would the momentum Democrats had gained in the state since 2018 suddenly erode? There was no way to tell, but one thing was certain, 2020 was here and the fight for the state's future was on.

RECAP

- Democratic gains in Arizona are put in jeopardy by the divisive impeachment issue.

- Despite supporting Trump's impeachment, the state party has to walk a fine line in order to maintain appeal from moderate voters.

- A possible Sinema no vote threatens to rile up the progressive base and create a public relations headache at the starting line of 2020.

- Right-wing animosity escalates to direct attacks on our office.

- We respond defiantly.

2

BATTLEGROUND

Election-year tactics are in full sway
and the stakes for the country
have never been higher

7

STATE OF WAR:
COMMUNICATIONS TACTICS IN
THE HEAT OF CAMPAIGN SEASON

The second we entered the New Year, the knives were out between the AZGOP and the Arizona Democratic Party. The year 2020 kicked off amidst the impeachment trial and fears of a war with Iran, given the assassination of the ruthless Iranian general Qasem Soleimani. Again, the Trump administration's foreign policy had put Americans in jeopardy. In Arizona we focused our efforts on making clear that, while we had no love for Soleimani, foreign policy demanded careful action in order to avoid unnecessary escalation. As for the ongoing issue of impeachment, we amplified the arguments for hearing from witnesses; specifically, shaming Arizona Republican lawmakers who were in favor of silencing witness testimony. Polling indicated that the majority of Arizonans wanted to hear from witnesses, even if they were not convinced that the president deserved removal from office.

On February 5, the trial ultimately concluded the way many had predicted: with an acquittal. But there was still some suspense. On the day the president was to be charged or acquitted on two articles of impeachment, we were unsure how Senator Sinema would vote, given her maverick brand.

The first state committee meeting of 2020 had occurred in January during the ongoing impeachment and featured an attempt by the progressives to pass a resolution advising Senator Sinema to vote in line with the Democratic Party. True to form, they had brought this effort back in January, as they had promised in September. But this time, the resolution's wording was changed from censure to advisement. When the press caught wind of this censure returning from the dead, the clarification that it was an advisement and not censure dampened their efforts to flood the zone with fresh material on the perceived spat between progressives and Sinema.

The advisory was tabled in committee and, therefore, the press was starved of an embarrassing rupture in the state Democratic Party at the opening of an election year.

However, in the event Sinema voted to acquit the president, there would be no guarantee that the entire state party would not turn on her and, as a result, effectively rebuke the first Democratic senator for Arizona elected in decades. Sinema had not disclosed or hinted to anyone in party leadership how she would vote. Needless to say, the press was relentless in their efforts to get a scoop. But mum was the word.

The suspense ended when Sinema finally voted to charge the president on both impeachment articles, effectively killing off momentum for an eventual censure and giving relief to worried Democrats. Not lost on me was the historical significance of the impeachment trial. The other dramatic moment of the day came from Senator Romney, who stood as the lone Republican to vote in favor of impeachment due to the evidence against the president. Senator Romney will go down in history as the only Republican with courage and conviction.

Our statement following Senator Sinema's vote:

For Immediate Release

Wednesday, February 5th, 2020

Contact: Matt Grodsky, mgrodsky@azdem.org

Arizona Democratic Party Statement: Courage & Conviction

Arizona Democratic Party Chair Felecia Rotellini issued the following statement considering Senator Sinema's vote for conviction on both articles of impeachment:

"Arizona Democrats commend Senator Sinema's vote for conviction on both articles of impeachment. We also appreciate her efforts to make this a fair trial. Senator Sinema honored her responsibility to enact impartial justice. She never committed to a decision until after she was presented with the evidence admitted at the impeachment trial and she pushed for witnesses to be included throughout this procedure.

"It is clear that Senator Sinema listened to the facts and made the right conclusion—the President broke the law and was derelict in his constitutional duty. Senator Sinema was not partisan, she was not predetermined, she was independent in her process—and we admire that. To impeach a President is a solemn responsibility, one that requires courage and conviction. Thank you, Senator Sinema, for bringing these virtues to the Senate. We intend to send more Democrats with those same qualities to Congress and the White House in November.

"The Arizona Democratic Party expresses our gratitude to our Democratic House Representatives for their diligent work and considerations throughout the impeachment of the President. Our Democratic Delegation never dismissed their duties to work for the people while this investigation was conducted—Democrats in the House helped to pass the USMCA, voted to lower the cost of prescription drugs, and reached a budget deal with Republicans that avoided a senseless shutdown.

"It is time now to focus on winning in 2020 and solving the issues impacting our state:

- Making sure everyone has affordable, accessible healthcare.
- Standing up for Medicare and Social Security.
- Fighting for a great public education system so every kid has a shot at the American dream.
- Working towards Smart Immigration Reform and giving DACA recipients a pathway to citizenship.
- Protecting our environment.
- Creating an economy that works for everyone.

"Arizona Democrats are united in their fight to ensure Arizona's 11 electoral votes go to our nominee for President, we are determined to elect Captain Mark Kelly and Democrats across the state, and we will not rest until we turn this state blue.

"We are proud of our Democratic representatives in Congress, now we march towards November."

✦ ✦ ✦

Amidst all of this, Arizona Democrats were also dealing with the recent revelation of Congresswoman Kirkpatrick's struggle with alcoholism. Congresswoman Kirkpatrick made the brave decision to check herself into a rehabilitation facility and spend a period of time away from Congress to deal with this issue, effectively opening the door for a Republican challenger in her upcoming House race and putting us back on defense two years after successfully gaining a majority in our congressional delegation. We managed this by issuing a statement of encouragement and support for the congresswoman. I was happy to see a lack of Republican attacks on her. Likely, the Republicans recognized going down that road would garner backlash. While most members of the media appreciated the congresswoman's situation, there were some who unfortunately wanted to spin this into some type of sensational hit-job. I worked quietly off the record to kill many of those inconsiderate stories but was unsuccessful in smothering all of them.

In case you haven't noticed by now, oftentimes in state parties there are multiple communications crises occurring all at once, and they are all in various stages of urgency. State party organizational leadership often does not understand that in the absence of adequate internal and external communications, operational response suffers, stakeholders go rogue, the organization will be perceived as inept, and the length of time required to bring full resolution to the issues will be extended. The basic steps of managing multiple communications crises require an ability to prioritize the issues at hand and minimize damage by not overreacting and making sure one spokesperson is issuing the messaging. Spoiler Alert: There will be more on managing crises in the next two chapters.

In spite of all of these simultaneous events, we still had a coalition to build. One of the most under-recognized voting groups is the

Asian American Pacific Islander population (AAPI).In the 2018 Asian American Voter Survey, 50% of Asian Americans received no contact or were unsure if they received contact about the election from the Democratic Party and 60% reported the same from the GOP, despite there being roughly 173,231 eligible AAPI voters in Arizona, with the majority of them residing in Maricopa County.

While our coordinated campaign worked to mobilize this vital demographic, ADP's political director and I met with Japan's consul general of the Southwestern United States, Akira Muto. The consul general had been appointed in 2019 and was working to gain an understanding of the Arizona Asian community from the perspective of both Republicans and Democrats. For us this represented an opportunity to cross-check our understanding of this community with individuals who actually represented them.

Our conversation centered primarily on economics. We discussed Arizona's trade partnerships, noting that Japan was Arizona's fourth-largest importer and the fifth-largest exporter for Arizona goods, representing a vital foreign market for Arizona farmers who were suffering under Trump's trade policies. Muto contended that while there was a dispute about trade policies, Republicans claimed that under Trump more jobs had been created than ever before. We were quick to counter by sharing that this was a false Republican talking point and that Trump had actually created fewer jobs. In fact, inTrump's first 36 months as president, the U.S. economy had gained 6.6 million jobs. But during a comparable 36-month period at the end of Obama's tenure, employers added 8.1 million jobs, or 23% more than what had been added since Trump took office.

It was evident that Muto was interested in gaining the perspectives of the political parties in Arizona so as to be better understand who he would be dealing with based on which party was victorious in November. As we continued to discuss outreach to Asian-Arizonans, I pointed out Arizona Democratic Party coverage in *Mainichi*, a large Japanese newspaper that enjoyed strong circulation in Arizona. I also discussed how we viewed Democratic values as American values, something we believed transcended demographics: affordable healthcare, an economy that works for everyone, and a flourishing education system. Muto appeared to agree and echoed that these were certainly values of Japanese Arizonans. Our political director also shared our plans to have several events with the AAPI caucus that would highlight AAPI candidates and mobilize those voters. At the meeting's conclusion, our key takeaway was that we needed to effectively educate AAPI voters on our values and cut through GOP misinformation, especially since this group had been neglected from outreach efforts for some time.

While the AAPI community was an important part of the coalition puzzle, we also needed to expand our outreach efforts with Latinx+Hispanic Arizonans, Native Americans, and African American Arizonans. The coordinated campaign would handle the ground game, and for the first time, the Arizona Democratic Party hired a Native American outreach manager and an African American outreach manager to drive engagement with these vital Arizonans. We also brought on a slew of Latinx+Hispanic-focused teams that spearheaded outreach on the coordinated campaign to engage that giant voting group across the state.

It was important for us to showcase our outreach efforts to the public and to the media as well. Since a state party's biggest critics are often its own members, we had to walk the walk, talk the talk, and let everyone know we were doing both.

For Immediate Release

Thursday, January 23, 2020

Contact: Matt Grodsky, mgrodsky@azdem.org

ICYMI: Arizona Democrats Put Early Organizing Focus On The Navajo Nation

PHOENIX — A report from the National Journal highlights the Arizona Democratic Party's ongoing efforts to invest in organizing, voter registration, and turnout in the Navajo Nation.

Key points from the *National Journal*:

- "The 170,000-person Navajo Nation, which stretches across the northeast corner of Arizona and into New Mexico and Utah, is a potential gold mine of Democratic votes. But in order to harness that political advantage, the Democratic Party is getting started earlier than ever to boost turnout."

- "Arizona is sure to be competitive in the presidential race and the Senate race, where retired astronaut Mark Kelly is the presumptive Democratic nominee to face Republican incumbent Martha McSally."

- "A Democratic Congressional Campaign Committee spokesperson said the committee has started its efforts in the district earlier than in 2018, and for the first time is hiring a dedicated organizer for Native voters that will be based in the district. The Arizona Democratic Party, meanwhile, told National Journal that it has also hired a staffer focusing on outreach to Native Americans."

♦ "Kelly's campaign said he has made two trips to Navajo Nation so far, including meeting with Navajo Nation President Jonathan Nez and attending the annual Navajo Nation Parade. State Democratic Party chairwoman Felecia Rotellini visited in the fall. And Kelly has the support of state Sen. Jamescita Peshlakai, who represents much of Navajo Nation and serves as his campaign treasurer."

"In 2020, Arizona Democrats are focused on early organizing in the Navajo Nation," said Matt Grodsky, ADP spokesperson. "For Democrats to win statewide, we are going to need to turn out voters on the Navajo Nation, and we recognize the importance of showing up, mobilizing voters, and talking to people about the issues that are important to them. That's why we're prioritizing voter registration and investing in staff earlier than ever before."

✦ ✦ ✦

Meanwhile, Republicans were stepping up their efforts in the state and reaching out to every demographic, too. A sea of Republican canvassers had descended on the 15 counties, working tirelessly to register voters. The strategy was to turn out Republicans who supported Trump in 2016 but had supposedly slept through the 2018 midterms. The idea was that re-engaging these voters would blunt the expected Democratic surge in 2020. In his State of the Union Address, Trump highlighted several guests from Arizona. Among them were a Tuskegee airman and his great-grandson, as well as parents of ISIS victim Kayla Mueller. This signaled to us that Trump was not just rattled about Arizona potentially slipping from his grasp, but it also showed us he wasn't just going to let us take it from him. Nothing made that clearer than when Trump announced he would be coming out to Arizona for a campaign rally on February 18, 2020. We knew that if Trump was headed to Arizona, we had to suck up the media airtime and starve him of attention. This would essentially be the opening salvo in the war for the state in 2020. We had to bracket him.

Quickly, what is bracketing? Great question. It is a communications tactic of scheduling local press events before and after an opponent's appearance in various media markets in order to dilute and mitigate the influence of the opponent's message so that you might earn coverage for your own candidate or cause. The tactic's origins are rooted in a 2002 meeting that was held in the White House between President Bush Political Director Ken Mehlman and RNC Regional Media Director Kevin Sheridan. The two were looking for ways to mess with the Democrats' presidential-primary season and decided on the idea of making news in a local media market immediately before and after a Democrat's stop there to counter the Democratic message.

Working with the DNC, we arranged for DNC Chairman Tom Perez to fly to Arizona to hold a press roundtable with Chair Rotellini, two members of Arizona's state Legislature, and everyday Arizonans who were positively impacted by the Affordable Care Act. This required immense logistical preparation and advance work. Advance is crucial for any press event. It is imperative that podiums are where they need to be, lights work, microphones are functioning, and that participants know where they need to be. Advance work is daunting, but luckily for me our chief of staff, Kelly Paisley, built her career on political advance work, having served in the Clinton and Obama administrations, so I had great support with her at my side.

The framing of the entire bracketing event was healthcare. Just the prior week, Trump had unveiled his 2021 budget proposal that called for colossal cuts to Medicare, Medicaid, and Social Security, all against the backdrop of a president who was backing a lawsuit to dismantle the Affordable Care Act while at the same time lying to Americans about working to protect coverage for their pre-existing conditions.

The Perez event would simply be the first wave of the week. On Tuesday we also slated Democratic State Representative Randy Freise to hold a press event featuring Arizona seniors whose healthcare would be in jeopardy should the Trump budget be approved. On Wednesday, as Trump flew to Arizona, we would blanket social media with anti-Trump messaging. Come Thursday, the day after the president's trip, we had devised a way to have the last word for the week.

Stacey Abrams, famed Georgia gubernatorial candidate from 2018, had agreed to fly to Arizona and advocate for protecting voter rights under the umbrella of her organization, Fair Fight. Using the Carpenter's Union Hall, a giant space in West Phoenix, Stacey addressed a room of 300+ people while flanked by Secretary Hobbs, Congressman Gallego, Felecia Rotellini, and State Representative Bolding. The crowd went wild as she discussed Arizona's battleground status and emphasized the importance of getting out the vote.

In my time with the state party, I had the opportunity to meet numerous public figures. I have to say that Stacey Abrams was among the kindest, most-down-to-earth individuals I ever met. While we waited in a stairwell after the event for the crowd to disperse and for the media to set up for a post-event gaggle, Ms. Abrams could tell I was a little stressed out after 12 hours of the event set up, execution, and now my attempts to keep her and her staff comfortable in our makeshift holding room. Ms. Abrams put her hand on my arm and said, "Don't you worry about me, I am just fine. Everything is just fine." She certainly did not have to do that and the fact that she did speaks volumes about her selfless character.

That week we successfully carved into the president's earned media opportunities and showed that Arizona was truly up for grabs. It helped us to develop our bracketing playbook for future Trump events in the state. Little did we know that everything was about to change.

RECAP

+ Senate Republicans acquitted Trump.

+ We focused on building our coalitions in underrepresented communities across Arizona that had traditionally been forgotten or taken for granted. This was a vital communications tactic. In a battleground state you need every voter you can possibly motivate to show up. They won't engage if they feel like you don't genuinely care about them.

+ There is an assumption that only the big-wigs in DC meet with stakeholders of foreign political entities, but our allies have their ambassadors, consuls, and officials stationed throughout the United States. They are all working to understand the political lay of the land in specific regions of the country since there are implications for their own countries. It's okay to engage with these individuals in official settings, as they can often help to amplify your message to their audiences.

+ Bracketing is now a hallmark of campaigns. It is designed to dilute the impact of an opponent's scheduled press event.

+ Advance preparation is hard work. Try to have experienced advance-team personnel on your staff or in your orbit to help you.

8

A PLAGUE O' BOTH OUR HOUSES: ADAPTING COMMUNICATIONS WHEN THE WORLD CHANGES

At the time of this writing, more than 500,000 Americans are dead and millions have been infected with what has come to be known as COVID-19, or the Coronavirus. Like so many American families, mine was not immune to the ravages of this disease, and sadly, we lost a member of our family early on in the crisis. Large swaths of Americans' jobs have vanished, their bank accounts emptied. Communities of color, from the Navajo Nation to Latinx+Hispanic Americans and African Americans, have been hit especially hard by the vicious nature of this disease. There is no aspect of American life that has not been transformed. As a result, the economy has tanked and, with it, countless peoples' hopes and dreams. While the vaccine effort is now underway, so many lives could have been saved had the Trump Administration acted competently early on and throughout the crisis. What's clear is that none of this colossal hardship and suffering should have been this bad; it could have been prevented.

In this chapter, I cover a few different situations that occurred during the onset of the virus, but I seek to emphasize just one major point: at our state party it was certainly easy for folks to get bogged down in the emergency of the moment and to dwell on one issue while neglecting several others. It's important not to fall into this trap. Unprecedented challenges happen. Sometimes, it is a misprinted campaign sign; sometimes, it is a global catastrophe. We don't get to choose. What is important is having the ability to adapt and recover. This is something we managed to execute well throughout the course of the year.

Game-changer

At the close of 2019, Americans had heard the news about a deadly epidemic racing through Asia. But with no alarms sounding from the top of the U.S. Government, the general public was left believing that this virus would somehow stay away from our homeland and not dare cross the two oceans that shielded us.

At the time, we didn't know about President Trump's malpractice when warned about the risks posed by the virus, and we certainly didn't fathom that it would shut down the country. But as we entered the month of March 2020, the virus was beginning to take center stage as it made landfall in the United States and started wreaking havoc.

Arizona was slated to host a Democratic Primary presidential debate in the days leading up to our Presidential Preference Election (PPE) in which voters would cast ballots that would assign the state's delegates to a specific candidate ahead of the Democratic National Convention. Having the debate in Arizona was a validator for us. For months we had been preaching Arizona's status as a battleground state, and having a debate scheduled for Phoenix helped drive that point home. When the announcement came down, the press sprang to life. Everyone wanted to talk to us about what the debate meant for our status as a swing state.

Notably, in early March Chair Rotellini sat down with acclaimed conservative *Washington Post* journalist George Will to discuss Arizona and our efforts to turn it blue. Despite conventional wisdom, it was a worthwhile risk for the chair to speak with George Will who was a renowned conservative journalist who had no love for Trump. Felecia would be able to provide crucial information to him about the Arizona electorate, not usually covered in national publications, and it would give us a chance to get our message across to a conservative yet amiable audience.

We were certainly focused on firing up Democrats and independents, but it was important that we meet with George Will to try and connect with Republicans who might be persuaded to buck their party and vote their conscience.

There were some who were weary of meeting with such a conservative stalwart in the world of journalism, but Felecia had a great meeting with George Will and his ultimate piece recapping the interview reflected that.

His piece was titled "A loose brick in Republicans' red wall" and included background about the chair, which undoubtedly made her relatable to readers unfamiliar with her, and it included important information that we wanted to get across about the state's voting history as well as our prospects in 2020. Notably, the article pointedly stated, "Speaking of walls, this year Trump will have to spend time and money to hold Arizona, another increasingly loose brick in the red wall that has protected Republicans' increasingly narrow path to 270 electoral votes. Two other such bricks are Texas and Georgia. Stay tuned."

Stay tuned, indeed. Super Tuesday had come and gone, so now the race looked to be between Vice President Biden and Senator Sanders. On the eve of the debate weekend, when candidates were supposed to arrive in Arizona and take the stage at the Arizona Federal Theater, the debate was canceled due to the sudden spike in COVID-19 cases.

Like a domino effect, sports seasons were canceled, the Olympic Games were postponed, the world ground to a halt. With the debate no longer a defining testament to our battleground status, our focus snapped to the upcoming Presidential Preference Election and how to ensure public safety amidst a deadly pandemic.

The cancelation of Arizona's presidential debate was the first wrench thrown into our campaign machine because of the pandemic, but it was not the last. As the threat of the virus became apparent, the Arizona Democratic Party and Mission for Arizona went fully virtual and halted in-person canvassing. This caused some obvious readjustments in the coordinated campaign's four-phase plan since they understandably never accounted for a global pandemic. As far as the PPE was concerned, we followed the lead of our secretary of state, Katie Hobbs, who announced that the election would proceed because the majority of voters had already cast their ballots by mail and because we didn't know when it would be safer to do this again since cases were projected to spike considerably. Her decision turned out to be the correct one, and election officials went above and beyond to make polling locations safe for the public.

On March 15, the day we were supposed to have our presidential debate, I went on MSNBC to discuss the Presidential Preference Election and the safety precautions underway to ensure public safety during an election that was now 48 hours away.

The interview was scheduled for 6 am Eastern time, which meant I had the luxury of being driven to the satellite studio just before 3 am. The interview lasted roughly three and a half minutes. Live, on air, Anchor Lindsey Rieser asked point-blank, "Do you concede that voters could be put at risk and what's the concern here? So many people showing up to vote that some potentially get exposed or so few showing up that numbers are down?"

"We are aware of the risk, and it's definitely top of mind. An encouraging thing that we have heard from election officials is that all polling locations will have extra soap, voting machines will be sanitized, there's going to be extra staff on hand to help with that. We are encouraged by what we're hearing," I replied.

I went on to thank our poll workers and spoke to the fact that there had been no exodus of polling-location personnel despite the risks posed by COVID-19. I also discussed the emergency voting period and the options voters had at their disposal to safely cast their ballots, "It's important their voices are heard. I do believe people are going to be protected."

Later on in the interview, Lindsey asked, "Logistics aside, let's talk about of course what's at stake in Arizona. Polls show Biden edging out Sanders in your state. Do you think there will be any surprises come Tuesday?"

"Hard to anticipate surprises," I replied, remembering that despite Biden's polling edge, it was important for us to not poke the eye of our progressive coalition. "I will tell you that both candidates are very popular with the Democratic Party in Arizona, both of them have strong name recognition, we have seen Joe Biden move up in the polls since Super Tuesday, and as I mentioned earlier, some sixty percent of Arizonans had held onto their ballots until after Super Tuesday. So it's very possible many of those voters broke for Biden, but we'll just have to wait and see. Either candidate could certainly win the state on Tuesday."

Super Tuesday Part Three

Two weeks after the initial Super Tuesday, and two days after my MSNBC appearance, our PPE was record-breaking. Early ballots alone exceeded the combined Democratic ballot totals from 2016. This was due to there being more Democrats in Arizona than four years prior and enthusiasm was up.

For Immediate Release

Tuesday, March 17th, 2020

Contact: Matt Grodsky, mgrodsky@azdem.org

Election Day Update: Early Vote Crushes 2016 PPE Total Vote Count

PHOENIX - The Arizona Democratic Party is confident that early ballots alone have exceeded the combined Democratic ballot totals from 2016.

2016

Total ballots cast in the 2016 Presidential Preference Election for Democrats were: 468,461

Early vote percentages in 2016 were 33%.

2020

Today there have been roughly 480,000 early ballots cast in this PPE for the Democratic candidates.

Roughly 39% of registered Democrats have voted early this year.

COVID-19

The public should continue to exercise caution but understand that polling centers have been properly equipped with the necessary items to ensure public safety. Election officials across the state have been working around the clock to help ensure that voting locations remain safe and accessible. Voters are urged to contribute to these efforts by:

- Washing hands often with soap and water for at least 20 seconds, both before and after visiting a voting location. If soap and water are not readily available, use an alcohol-based hand sanitizer.

- Keeping 4 to 6 feet from other people when at the voting location.

- Not touching your face with unwashed hands.

- Covering your cough or sneeze with a tissue, and discarding the tissue in the trash.

INFO FOR VOTERS

If voters have election day related questions, they are encouraged to call our hotline all day until polls close at 7 pm: **1-833-VOTE-4-AZ**

"As we expected, the early ballot surge has allowed us to beat 2016 voter turnout levels," said Matt Grodsky, spokesman for the Arizona Democratic Party, "We will know in-person voting numbers at a later time, but are thrilled at the number of early ballots that were cast. Democrats are energized and determined to beat this President in November," he added.

✦ ✦ ✦

The secretary of state's decision to proceed with the PPE turned out to be the smartest call, considering how COVID-19 would wreak havoc on Arizona in the months to come and that thousands of Arizonans had already voted by mail. The *New York Times* reported: "In Arizona, the state Democratic Party was seeing huge turnout in the form of early mail-in ballots," said Matt Grodsky, a party spokesman. "We believe that delaying the election would cause undue chaos to this election process," he said. Katie Hobbs, Arizona's secretary of state, said that "we have no guarantee that there will be a safer time to hold this election in the near future," adding, "The longer we wait, the more difficult and dangerous it could become."

The results from our PPE yielded a Biden victory, continuing his Super Tuesday momentum and essentially locking down the nomination.Biden made an appeal in the wake of his sweeping victory on March 17, a victory that included winning the state of Arizona and effectively putting Senator Sanders out of reach for the nomination. Sanders had held a lead in Arizona polls ahead of Super Tuesday but had since fallen behind. "Senator Sanders and I may disagree on tactics, but we share a common vision for the need to provide affordable health-care for all Americans, reducing income inequality that has risen so drastically, to tackling the existential threat of our time: climate change. Senator Sanders and his supporters have brought a remarkable passion and tenacity to all of these issues, and together they have shifted the fundamental conversation in this country. So let me say, especially to the young voters who have been inspired by Senator Sanders, I hear you, I know what's at stake. I know what we have to do. Our goal as a campaign and my goal as a candidate for president is to unify this party and then to unify the nation. You know, it's in moments like these we realize we need to put politics aside and work together as Americans."

The voters had spoken; it was decisive and it was clear. Joe Biden would be the nominee for president, and many of us were certain he could defeat Trump. In fact most of the shifting towards Biden had been because voters wanted someone who they thought could beat the president. We watched this play out over the following months as additional primaries revealed that all across the country Democrats were compromising on ideological purity in favor of someone they thought could win.

Despite this appearing to be simple, we still had to communicate to our entire state party that we were neutral throughout the primary process and that it was important for everyone to come together once a nominee was formally chosen by the delegates at the party's convention. With the PPE behind us, our attention would soon be focused on the lengthy delegate selection process ahead of the July convention. But as the world was unraveling due to COVID-19, we soon learned that the convention was being postponed until August 17.

We were also informed that the normal way of selecting delegates would have to be reinvented with social distancing in mind. Complicating matters further, a bad actor successfully hacked our party website, forcing us to take unprecedented measures in our state party's history to lock down our website and invest heavily in cybersecurity for the remainder of the election.

Sometimes You Just Need to Call Someone Out

Shortly after the PPE, COVID-19 cases began to spike in Arizona. Despite the disease not caring if its victims were Republicans or Democrats, the pandemic quickly became a partisan issue. Instead of facing facts, right-wing protesters took to the streets to decry safety procedures as tyranny. In response, overwhelmed nurses counter-protested to raise awareness about the seriousness of COVID and their work on the front lines. This prompted AZGOP Chair and supposed primary care physician Kelli Ward to falsely Tweet that the ICU workers were just actors. That drew my ire and I released a statement attributed to me that read, "If anyone's status as a healthcare professional should be questioned it's Dr. Kelli Ward's considering her unwillingness to promote the advice of health experts. Irresponsible, shameful tweets like this do nothing to help people afflicted with the virus or the healthcare heroes who are working to save lives. Across Arizona, healthcare workers have been working tirelessly to take care of our most vulnerable and individuals afflicted with COVID-19. These heroes deserve our total and complete gratitude."

In what seemed like an effort to one-up each other with moronic statements, Arizona's GOP elected officials began saying the dumbest things. In retrospect I think the grand prize for idiotic statements should go to Congressman Andy Biggs. Biggs, a right-wing fanatic representing Arizona's 5th Congressional District, argued for reopening the economy, flouting CDC guidelines, firing Dr. Anthony Fauci, and allowing the public to try hydroxychloroquine, a drug not proven to have any effect in treating COVID-19. Biggs infamously voted against every COVID-19 relief bill in Congress. Slamming Biggs basically became my part-time job over the course of the summer. In one instance the *Arizona Mirror* reported:

In speeches and op-eds over the past month, Biggs has ripped into the federal and state government's response to COVID-19—including stay-at-home orders that are backed by President Donald Trump, like the one issued by Gov. Doug Ducey. On the House floor Thursday, Biggs called on U.S. governors "to free their citizens immediately." […] "He's out of touch with the situation and appears more interested in risking Arizonans' lives than improving them," Arizona Democratic Party spokesman Matt Grodsky said in a statement. "Voters will remember in November."

Sometimes, it can be a distraction to publicly call out someone who makes asinine comments. At times they want you to engage because it gives them the attention they desire, but in other instances it can make you look too trigger-happy and lacking in discipline. This is a careful dance, and while I often had to pick and choose my moments for when to hit members of the other party, I typically had no qualms about doing so when the issues at hand were as clear cut as respecting front-line workers and public safety.

What's Next?

As summer drew to a close, the cavalry was on its way. The Biden campaign and the DNC were quickly deploying staff to Arizona. Within days we had a Biden for Arizona state director and an entirely new ecosystem to coordinate with. We spent the entire month of July finalizing our delegate selection process, preparing for the virtual convention, and getting in sync with our new counterparts on Team Biden.

We also had a rapidly approaching primary on August 4 that would determine our down-ballot nominees across the state. Needless to say, all of these converging elements presented unique challenges, on top of the fact that we had an election going on that was unlike any other in American history. But as July neared its end, new challenges were on the horizon.

RECAP

- COVID-19 changed the landscape of the campaign and threw a wrench in much of our high-profile events.
- With the world changing around us and new challenges springing up daily, it was important for us and remains important for other state parties to remain nimble and roll with the punches.

9

ACT OF TERROR: COMMUNICATING IN A CRISIS

In a brief conversation with Sheriff Penzone in the early days of 2020, I indicated to the sheriff that I had some concerns about our office's vulnerability. The sheriff minced no words when he said that 2020 would bring out bad actors. From right-wing hate groups to disturbed lone wolves with no ideological loyalty, the sheriff was convinced that some people would take it upon themselves to wreak havoc on their perceived enemies.

Shortly after midnight on July 24, a previously banned volunteer for the Maricopa County Democratic Party drove up to our party headquarters, which housed both the ADP and the Maricopa County Democratic Party. The assailant calmly got out of his car outside the Maricopa County entrance, lit an incendiary device, and threw it into the office.

The blaze rapidly consumed nearly all of the county party's facility. Fireproof doors between the county office and ADP headquarters prevented the flames from overtaking our office; however, they could not repel the smoke and the fire's vicious assault through the ceiling. In a normal election year, it would have been highly likely that staff could have been working at the office at this hour. However, due to COVID-19, we were under a work-from-home policy, and therefore, no one was injured at the office.

Police and fire crews arrived almost immediately, and our office managers were quickly called to the scene. I was notified around roughly three in the morning that the building had caught fire. At the time, we did not know it was arson, but we certainly suspected foul play. However, I instructed our county party officials and members of our staff to refrain from any public speculation.

Crisis

The word crisis is borrowed from Latin, which in turn was borrowed from the Greek word *krisis*. The noun derived from the verb *krinō*, which means "**distinguish, choose, decide.**" After all, a crisis is just a set of decisions that can either solve or worsen a challenging situation.

After the building was vandalized in December 2019, I had unceremoniously thought up plans for how to respond in the event of a broader office crisis. In my mind that looked like a mass-shooting attempt or vandalism on a broader scale. I should have printed out a thorough playbook, laminated the damn thing, and kept it handcuffed to our team at all times; alas, sometimes politics moves too quickly. Nevertheless, I had a rough idea of what our plan should look like, considering my previous experiences representing public and private organizations.

Crisis plans formulate around several hypothetical questions, most pertinently: What are the circumstances? Who should respond? What should we avoid? When a crisis presents itself, there is often a tendency to overreact. It's vital to gather the facts and then consider how and why audiences are affected by the situation.

I knew immediately we would have members of the party jumping to conclusions and giving a hungry press fodder to speculate. Sometimes when a crisis occurs, the reasons aren't always obvious, and in some cases what seems obvious is actually much more complex.

Communicating a Crime Scene

Shortly after eight in the morning, I drove down to the headquarters. Knowing the media was inbound, I dictated communications to party members as I wove through traffic. I explained to folks that it was vital for us to acknowledge the heartbreak of the office's destruction, emphasize that no one was hurt, and not speculate on the fire's cause.

As I neared the building, I saw several television crews already on-site. Parking the car, I saw for the first time the wreckage spilling out of the Maricopa County side of the structure. Black ash and debris were smattered in front of the building's entryway, and the smell of burnt wood and furniture hung in the air.

I met the chief of staff and the chair in front of the building. Fire crews and police had created a perimeter around the building as they began their investigation. The chair and I spoke to several members of the media, explaining that our building had caught fire the previous night and that we had been in the building since the early 2000s. At this point in time, we feared the building would be a complete loss.

By midday, ATF was on-site, which only further validated our suspicions of arson. The Secret Service was also made aware of the incident. Sure enough, by the end of the day, police had determined that the fire had indeed been deliberately started. I stood off-camera as Felecia held a brief press conference explaining that this was now an arson investigation but that we would not be speculating on motive.

After her remarks we were able to enter the wreckage for the first time. We were warned to spend as little time as possible in the building, due to the damage and concerns over asbestos. Stepping into the ruin, our eyes immediately watered from the sting of smoke. Luckily, our COVID-19 masks helped to keep us somewhat protected from breathing the toxic air. The Maricopa County side of the office was completely obliterated. Throughout the rest of the office, smoke and water damage from the fire crew's valiant efforts had resulted in the entire structure being a total loss.

Our immediate concern turned to decades of memorabilia that would need to be immediately salvaged. I was able to gain access to my office and found that everything was intact. Something I will always remember is the heat impressions left on my desk and table surfaces. The heat had been so intense throughout the space that papers, mouse pads, and binders left on surfaces had created imprints of themselves on the face of the furniture. I salvaged a photo of my wife and me at our wedding, a canvas of her and our dog Kirby, and the American flag I had draped on my wall.

In the days that followed, there were some who wanted us to be calling every national news organization in the country—as if they weren't already calling us—to try to milk this story as a hate crime, no doubt executed by some fanatical Trump supporter.

Despite the drumbeat from some of these reactionaries, party leadership remained disciplined. We would not jump to conclusions. I Tweeted from my account: The Arizona Democratic Party will not comment on motives or methods in the arson investigation until law enforcement makes their determination. We lost our building. We will win the election.

It Takes a Village

As the investigation continued, it became indisputable that we could not return to work in the office ever again. The outpouring of support from people across Arizona and the country was remarkable. Within hours of news of the fire breaking, people were contacting us, trying to find ways to donate. We began a fund to help us gain the money needed to find a new space. In a year that had seen our economy collapse, when a global pandemic was wreaking havoc, people from all walks of life graciously donated money, space, and equipment to our staff. I will be forever grateful for their generosity.

Within just a few days, the vehicle from the video footage at the time of the fire was identified and the arsonist was ultimately arrested in Peoria. The arsonist was not the Trump-supporter boogeyman that many were certainly hoping for. He turned out to be a registered Democrat who was a former volunteer for the Maricopa County Democratic Party but had been banned due to his disturbing behaviors. The arsonist also claimed to have had an intimate relationship with Ivanka Trump and considered himself to be in the running for the GOP's vice presidential nominee. Numerous reports documented his deranged ramblings on social media and previous run-ins with political leaders. I found this to be evidence of an individual clearly suffering from mental illness.

Sticking to a strategy of calm and clarity, we issued a statement acknowledging the arrest and thanked first responders for their work. But the main point of our message was that we were not deterred and would remain focused on November.

Throughout this entire ordeal, I received outstanding support and encouragement from my communications colleagues on the Biden team and the coordinated campaign. At 26 years old, I had never dealt with a crisis quite like this one that had so many challenging layers and stakeholders. Having a helping hand from folks I had only been working with for a short time was a colossal relief.

Fall of Titans

Amidst all the turmoil and officially cementing 2020 as a terrible year were the devastating one-two punches of losing larger-than-life bastions of the civil rights movement and social justice. On the night of Friday, July 17, the country learned of the untimely passing of Congressman John Lewis, whose years of good trouble and selfless service helped bend the arc of this nation's history toward justice. Barely two months later, on September 18, another Friday evening, the notorious Justice Ruth Bader Ginsburg succumbed to cancer and passed into legend. The statements we issued in the wake of their deaths were some of the most heart wrenching I ever had to work on at that point. Congressman Lewis's death tore at the country's festering wound brought on by the George Floyd protests, while Justice Ginsburg's passing exacerbated the already dire concerns about the makeup of the Supreme Court. The implications for replacing her with a conservative justice suddenly threw substantially more pressure to the Arizona Senate race, given the possibility that the winner of the election would have to cast a vote for the nominee. With a battle for the court now a central issue, the already astronomical stakes for the upcoming election had been raised. As an important note to communications professionals, I advise getting proficient at writing statements in the aftermath of an elected official or an iconic person passing. This happened numerous times throughout my tenure and they are always difficult to write.

RECAP

- Always have a plan for dealing with a crisis. When one occurs, don't jump to conclusions or get swept up in the emotion of the situation.

- Everyone with a stake in your organization will have opinions. Some are good and should be considered, some suck. It's important not to get dragged down into the mess of "What I would do in this situation…" or "You should do this." There's a reason you're the communications person and they're not. The ball game is yours.

- Don't try too hard to be perfect. A crisis is a crisis for a reason, and there's no benefit in pretending that you're immune to its impacts. Rather than trying to shrug away the challenges at hand, acknowledge the situation,connect with all the parties involved, and articulate the next steps forward.

- Within a span of two months, the world lost Congressman John Lewis and Justice Ruth Bader Ginsburg. These devastating blows for democracy further raised the stakes for the election. As a communications professional, get good at writing mournful condolence statements. I wrote numerous ones during my tenure and the ones pertaining to the two aforementioned leaders were the most challenging during the election.

10

HOMESTRETCH: THE MOST CRUCIAL PERIOD FOR STATE PARTY COMMS

T he show had to go on, and so, come August 4, we held our Democratic primary. Despite a global pandemic and a new voting process in Arizona's most populous county, more than one million Arizonans cast ballots in the primary election. It was a crucial test-run for the November election and a helpful indicator for what things would look like in just three months.

The Primary

In the U.S. Congress, Arizona incumbents staved off their challengers. In races for the state Legislature, most sitting senators and representatives appeared to be successfully defending their seats. In Maricopa County, the frontrunner in the Democratic primary for county attorney, Julie Gunnigle, held a comfortable lead. But Incumbent Treasurer Royce Flora trailed his challenger, Republican state lawmaker John Allen.

Former Maricopa County Sheriff Joe Arpaio gave Jerry Sheridan, his former deputy chief, a tough fight in a four-way Republican Primary race for the county's top law enforcement job. After a few days of counting votes, Sheridan secured a slim win over Arpaio and would become a top target for the Arizona Democratic Party in the months that followed, where we drew attention to his corrupt record at the sheriff's office under Arpaio. The defeat of Arpaio was an important bellwether for Arizona's most consequential county, and his tenure with the sheriff's office had been the spark that ignited a decade of activism that propelled Democrats to a competitive position.

While Arpaio's defeat was a good sign, he had lost to his former number two and someone who was arguably just as corrupt and nefarious as the former sheriff. Sheridan would now face off against a Democratic incumbent in Sheriff Penzone. Given Sheridan's fledgling name recognition, it would be crucial that Democrats define him and tie the former deputy to the corruption of the Arpaio years or risk Penzone losing to an unknown quantity.

As reported in *The Hill* on August 7, 2020:

> "With the primary race for Maricopa County sheriff officially concluding tonight, Arizona Democrats reaffirm our commitment to protecting the Latino community from the likes of Joe Arpaio's former number two, Jerry Sheridan, who was found in contempt of court and will double down on Arpaio's disturbing legacy that embarrassed our state and cost taxpayers millions of dollars," said Matt Grodsky, spokesman for the Arizona Democratic Party. "Arizona's largest county is better off under the leadership of Sheriff Penzone, a leader with a legacy of accountability, committed to building community trust," he added. "We know voters will stick with him this November."

We had good news to communicate after the primary, which was a nice change from the recent turmoil of July. Tuesday's results had broad implications at every level of government. Democrats were poised to gain control of key congressional districts and flip the state Legislature. Republicans were vying to maintain control of both legislative chambers and hold their congressional seats.

Speaking of congressional seats, Democrats had an important decision to make in the Republican-leaning 6th Congressional District. Four Democrats were vying for the nomination and the right to challenge U.S. Representative David Schweikert, who was bogged down in a House Ethics Committee investigation over alleged misspending by his campaign and his office.

Physician Dr. Hiral Tipirneni won out over tech executive Anita Malik and business owners Karl Gentles and Stephanie Rimmer. In the Tucson-based 2nd Congressional District,incumbent Representative Ann Kirkpatrick beat Peter Quilter, who was making his first bid for office in the primary. In the 4th Congressional District, longtime Republican Congressman Paul Gosar handily prevailed over his challenger.

Though fewer Arizonans voted in person than in past primaries, the number of mail-in and early ballots exceeded total vote counts from the 2016 and 2018 primary elections. A change in state law allowed election officials to start tallying incoming ballots 14 days before Tuesday's primary rather than the usual 7 days.

Living History

As we moved past the primary, we became fully plugged in with the Biden campaign in Arizona. Our communications team was led by the Biden campaign's Arizona communications director, Geoff Burgan, a veteran communications professional based out of DC. The Biden team in Arizona was outstanding to work with and made genuine efforts to sync up with operatives in the state party who had been on the ground in Arizona for past cycles. As the Biden camp was transitioning into our operation, we watched history being made on August 11 as Senator

Kamala Harris of California was tapped as Biden's running mate, making her the first woman, African/South Asian American to be a vice-presidential nominee.

The official announcement for Harris's selection as the VP nominee came while Mike Pence was in Arizona for a campaign event; it was the ultimate bracketing success. I had been a big Harris fan since the close of 2016 and was thrilled to see her jump into the presidential primary. Having Harris on the ticket immediately electrified Democrats in Arizona and aligned liberals and moderates. *The Arizona Republic* reported:

Rep. Ruben Gallego, D-Ariz., one of the more outspoken liberals on Capitol Hill, has been a friend to Harris, D-Calif., for years and campaigned with her during her own presidential campaign last year. Grant Woods, the former Republican Arizona attorney general who switched parties to become a centrist-minded Democrat, is pleased to see someone who comes from a law enforcement background and reinforces Biden's own moderation.

With Harris on the ticket, I felt that our "Goldilocks" approach to Arizona would be bolstered. Her selection would help us continue to thread the needle between the left-and center-right Republicans. On a personal note, her groundbreaking selection as the vice-presidential nominee was a proud moment in our household, considering my wife was born in New Delhi, India, and shares Harris's ethnicity.

Throughout her career, Harris has managed to have one foot in progressive politics while keeping the other firmly placed in the center. While not the darling of the left like Bernie Sanders or Elizabeth Warren, and not a staunch blue-dog Democrat like Joe Manchin, Harris has championed progressive policies through pragmatic tactics, a strategy that has successfully mitigated significant alienation from core constituents in every office she has held. At the time of her selection, Harris was the only candidate on either major-party ticket with a net favorability rating that was positive. Within days, polls showed that Biden was getting high marks for picking Harris. The ABC News/ *Washington Post* poll indicated that 54% of Americans approved of the Harris selection as opposed to 29% disapproving. Democrats overwhelmingly approved of the pick by an 86% to 8% margin, as did independents with 52% to 29%. Our statement following the announcement of Senator Harris was one of the proudest statements I ever had the privilege of helping to craft (I bought my Biden-Harris yard sign as I was typing the release):

For Immediate Release

Tuesday, August 11, 2020

Contact: Matt Grodsky, mgrodsky@azdem.org

Arizona Democratic Party Statement On The Biden-Harris Ticket

Chair Felecia Rotellini issued the following statement:

"Arizona Democrats are thrilled to learn of Vice President Joe Biden's choice for his running mate in this historic election, Senator Kamala Harris.

"As the Senator of America's largest state, Senator Harris is ready to lead on Day One. She shares Joe Biden's bedrock beliefs of standing up for all Americans and especially working families, and she is a proven fighter for the middle class.

"As the former Attorney General of California, a lifelong civil rights leader, a Senator, and strong Presidential candidate, she is ready to be the Vice President of the United States.

"Senator Harris has always recognized Arizona's importance as an emerging battleground state. She was a **vital supporter** of our success in 2018 when Arizonans elected four Democratic women to statewide office.

"The Arizona Democratic Party is committed to doing everything in its power to send Arizona's eleven electoral votes to the Biden-Harris ticket and restore integrity to the White House this November."

✦ ✦ ✦

Re-inventing Campaigning

Throughout the final sprint of the election, another challenge we were reckoning with was the inability to hold mass gatherings amidst the pandemic. Following the lead of the Biden campaign, we relied heavily on virtual meetings and fundraising events, whereas Trump's campaign held in-person events without regard for public health. The president held seven events in the state in 2020.

The Biden campaign and the Arizona Democratic Party were aided by celebrities such as America Ferrera, Kerry Washington, Cher, Mark Ruffalo, Jessica Alba, and Jennifer Garner. Biden held one event after the Democratic National Convention over the summer, a bus tour around Maricopa County in October, that served as his and Senator Harris's first joint-campaign event. Senator Harris returned to Arizona in October for an in-person, socially distanced event.

There was constant criticism that the vice president and senator were not coming to Arizona enough, but what we found was that Arizonans in rural counties who normally couldn't access these types of events finally had a way to do so. Arguably, the virtual nature of this campaign season allowed us to reach more people than we perhaps would have in a normal year, and despite the turmoil sweeping the nation, Biden was maintaining a steady edge in polling, including in Arizona.

This explained why Trump, who only won Arizona by a meager four points, made numerous visits to Arizona. When he couldn't come, he sent Vice President Pence as his top surrogate. This certainly increased our need for bracketing events. Every other week it seemed as though we were counter-messaging Mike Pence or Trump as they held reckless rallies across the state.

Black Lives Matter and Striking the Right Tone

In 2015 *The Washington Post* started logging every fatal shooting by an on-duty police officer in the U.S. Nearly 1,000 people were shot and killed by police in 2020. Based on the country's population breakdown by race, black Americans are shot and killed by police at a disproportionately higher rate when compared to white Americans.

In the first months of 2020, black Americans were once again being killed at the hands of police, and tensions were slowly beginning to rise. In March 2020, Breonna Taylor was needlessly gunned down by police executing a no-knock search warrant in Kentucky. One month prior, in Georgia, a 25 year-old black man named Ahmaud Arbery was savagely hunted by three white men and shot point blank for the crime of jogging. While his murderers were immediately identified in a disturbing, 36-second video that showed an unarmed Arbery being gunned down like an animal, it took months for police to make arrests. It would be 74 days before the suspects were charged. Then in May came the tragic murder of George Floyd.

George Floyd, another unarmed black man, was murdered while handcuffed and pinned to the ground by officer Derek Chauvin's knee in an episode that was captured on video, igniting worldwide protests. It wouldn't be the last tragedy that summer. The death of Dion Johnson and the shooting of Jacob Blake soon followed as did similar incidents across the country that only heightened tensions. As summer drew to a close, one of the immediate elements we had to consider in our communications strategy was how to address the racial tensions sweeping the nation.

The grotesque murder of Floyd had created a groundswell of refreshed activism across the country. Finally, it seemed like the Black Lives Matter movement was becoming mainstream. Leaders were saying it with pride, professional sports teams were brandishing it, and lawmakers were taking action in the form of meaningful legislation. Democrats in the U.S. House passed the "George Floyd" police reform bill and state legislatures across the country took up the call to change their law enforcement organizations for the better. Most importantly, Floyd's death was uniting people of the left and the right in their shared belief that what was happening was just plain wrong.

We moved quickly to further enhance our efforts to shine a light on racial injustice, and we clearly communicated our support of Democrats in the state Legislature who wanted to hold a special session to address police reform. Further exacerbating the desire for a reckoning over racial injustice in Arizona, was the death of another African American male at the hands of law enforcement. Dion Johnson was killed during an arrest in Phoenix on May 25 after being pulled over by DPS officers. The Republican county attorney refused to pursue charges against the officer who killed Johnson.

Where the party as a whole hit a snag was the unfortunate Defund the Police rhetoric. The original meaning of the phrase, as defined in Good Housekeeping, was: *reducing police department budgets and redistributing those funds towards essential social services that are often underfunded, such as housing, education, employment, mental healthcare, and youth services.*

The introduction of the phrase into the public sphere and its subsequent evolution into a right-wing lightning rod brought back my memories of the 2018 midterms when an Abolish ICE movement found its way into Democratic talking points and caused damage to progressive candidates in battleground states. Arizonans by and large did not support such an idea. For instance, when David Garcia, the Arizona gubernatorial candidate in 2018, waded in on the issue and called for the less drastic plan of "replacing ICE with an immigration system that reflects our American values," he was tied to the abolish movement by Republicans, and it arguably hurt him considerably in the race. Sinema, by contrast, never fell into the abolish trap.

Now here we were again with another controversial law enforcement phrase that was poised to throw a wrench into our messaging. Nevertheless, some on the left used the phrase proudly, and like clockwork, conservatives seized on it as evidence of radical leftism and used it to enhance ridiculous but effective advertisements they had already been injecting into the American bloodstream. One outlandish ad campaign showed unanswered 911 calls and chaos in the streets. Regardless of one's position on the phrase, it was a moment that required us to once again thread the messaging needle.

We had to strike a constant balance of highlighting Black Lives Matter and pushing for police reform without falling into the trap of the "defund" rhetoric, which was alienating moderate voters. Having represented law enforcement organizations in the midst of policing reforms, I had experience messaging these types of issues to the public, and thankfully, the Arizona Biden team had a well thought out strategy.

The tone we struck was honest and one that I wholeheartedly believe should be the message nationwide. It essentially leveraged the Elaboration Likelihood Model, a theory of communication that centers on the idea that if a person cares about an issue being communicated to them, and if they have regular access to that message, then that person will elaborate on the message in their community. Lasting persuasion is achieved when the receiver thinks or rehearses favorable thoughts about the message.

Ever the battleground state, we had to carefully position it within our message framework. We settled on this theme of messaging: All of these things are true at once. Black Lives Matter and the majority of law enforcement professionals are good people who want to serve their communities, but bad actors exist, and they must be rooted out and brought to justice. There are systemic, racist issues in law enforcement that have contributed to generations of injustice upon communities of color that must be reformed.

At the chair's instinctive direction, I took on the effort to create a landing page on the Arizona Democratic Party's website devoted entirely to Black Lives Matter. I worked with the chair, the African American outreach manager, one of our vice-chairs who was an activist in the African American community, and our political director, to provide resources and content on the page that explained the pervasive issues facing African Americans and challenged visitors to expand their understanding of the history of racial injustice in America. Communications professionals in other battleground states should consider such a measure for their state party websites, constituents and stakeholders want resources and messaging guidance. Oftentimes, landing pages on your website are the most convenient way to talk to your voters and give them the necessary information to share in the community.

Black Lives Matter and the struggle to get some Americans to recognize that indisputable truth goes on. Ahead of the 2022 midterms, the 2024 election, and I fear still in years to come, there will be more

George Floyds. Democrats have taken firm positions on policing reform and resolving these systemic injustices, it is important for state parties to hone messaging around these vital issues and address them regularly as well as in moments of national reckoning. It will help to sharpen defenses against right-wing spin and advance needed change.

RECAP

- The completion of the August primary brought us to the final stretch of the election. All Democrat U.S. House incumbents handily won their elections.

- "Defund the Police" rhetoric complicated messaging around the need for reforms and change that was advancing in the wake of George Floyd's murder. We initiated a communications balancing act for our battleground state that sought to avoid falling into GOP traps without alienating Democrats.

- We had to rely on virtual campaign events due to COVID-19. This helped us realize that individuals across Arizona who normally would not have access to key events were now able to because of the inclusive, virtual nature of the events.

- Create issue-based landing pages that are easily accessible to the public. This can help amplify your message.

- Communicate positions and policy on important issues around race and policing reform regularly as it will blunt GOP spin and advance just causes.

11

DUE SEASON: COMMUNICATING ON ELECTION NIGHT AND BEYOND

"This loss hurts, but please never stop believing that fighting for what's right is worth it. It is worth it. And so we need you to keep up these fights now and for the rest of your lives. I believe we are stronger together and we will go forward together. And you should never, ever regret fighting for that. Scripture tells us, 'Let us not grow weary in doing good, for in due season, we shall reap if we do not lose heart.' So my friends, let us have faith in each other, let us not grow weary, let us not lose heart, for there are more seasons to come. And there is more work to do. I am incredibly honored and grateful to have had this chance to represent all of you in this consequential election. May God bless you and may God bless the United States of America."

I couldn't help but think of Secretary Clinton's concession speech. Everything we had done since November 9, 2016, had led us to this historic moment, a crossroads in history where the nation would choose either fascism or the restoration of dignity and integrity to our government. I thought of the note I had written to myself as Clinton conceded the election: *Remember this moment. Remember how you feel. Do something so that you never feel this way again.*

We were hunkered down in an office in downtown Phoenix, a space temporarily gifted to us considering our office situation. While the majority of the staff was social distancing throughout the building, I was in the back with the chair and chief of staff, fielding virtual press inquiries where we focused on expressing cautious optimism.

In order to win the U.S. presidential election, a candidate must win in enough states to have 270 Electoral College votes. Polls closed in Arizona at 7 pm in the wake of Florida and Texas, breaking Trump's way and fueling the Democrats' 2016 PTSD. But Arizona proved to be the firewall we had long argued it could be. Early on in the night, the surge of early mail-in votes, which were expected to lean Democratic, broke our way. The narrative quickly changed from Trump's early election night to success to Arizona being the first state to flip. Our initial numbers were so good that many believed we had swept a number of races across Maricopa County, secured the Senate race, and delivered the 11 electoral votes to Biden.

But we had to keep the champagne on ice. Mail-in ballots are counted first and the in person Election Day votes would likely favor Republicans. It would be an emotional roller coaster. To our surprise, Fox News was the only network to call Arizona for Biden on election night. Despite catching flak from the RNC and the Trump campaign, the network stuck to its guns. Arnon Mishkin, director of the Fox

News Decision Desk, said the network was confident in its statistical model projecting Biden the winner. "We're four standard deviations from being wrong," Mishkin said. "And, I'm sorry, we're not wrong in this particular case." I had never been so happy with a Fox News report in my life. Soon afterward, the *Associated Press*, which is the grand-daddy of election results, called Arizona for Biden.

The AP's subsequent piece after the call read in part: Joe Biden won Arizona's 11 electoral votes, becoming the second Democratic presidential candidate since 1948 to claim victory in the longtime-Republican stronghold. The former vice president benefited from the state's changing demographics and successfully won over swing voters who split their tickets two years ago to elect a Republican governor and a Democrat to the U.S. Senate.

Mathematically, the number-crunchers were seeing the same data we were seeing. While Trump would make up ground in the state, he was unlikely to catch Biden once all the votes were tallied. Despite the reassuring calls from Fox and AP, other networks and organizations were not as eager to make a definitive call and they opted to wait until more results came in. Knowing we were in for a long counting process, we wrapped the chair's interviews and cleared out for the night.

Election night ended without a clear winner, as many state results were too close to call and millions of votes remained uncounted, including in the battleground states of Wisconsin, Michigan, Pennsylvania, North Carolina, Georgia, Nevada, and Arizona. Results were delayed in these states due to local rules on counting mail-in ballots, something that the public had been informed about at nauseam for at least six months. At three am, I was still awake and glued to the television. Biden had picked up 224 electoral votes versus 213 for Trump. Despite Biden's narrow lead, Trump tried to prematurely claim victory in an address to supporters, but millions of legally cast ballots were still being counted.

While we didn't get a definitive call on election night, and while we were confident that Arizona would remain in Biden's column despite the shyness of some networks to call it, I didn't want us to seem overly cocky or ahead of the game. We scrapped interviews and statements for the remainder of the night. Any communication to the press going forward would reiterate our confidence in Arizona being blue without delving into long winded explanations on the number of outstanding ballots that needed to be counted and various mathematical scenarios. In our hearts we knew that history had been made, and I knew that I had done what was necessary to help us turn Arizona blue. I could tell my future children that, in this moment of crisis, I took action and played a small part in helping Democrats achieve the impossible.

RECAP

- On election nights, buckle up and stay calm. Anything can happen.

- Don't get ahead of yourselves with overly confident statements or decorations to the press. It is typically better to stay quiet and await results rather than having to retract something later on. Voicing optimism is different from voicing certainty.

- The AP's call is generally considered the rubber stamp of results on election night.

- Be patient.

12

AFTERMATH: MESSAGING AND STRATEGY ASSESSMENTS

J oe Biden was named the projected winner for the presidential election on November 7, 2020. I didn't see the official call from the networks. I had gone down to our temporary office to prepare the space for inevitable interviews our chair would have to do once the announcement was made. Upon arriving at the office, I became pre-occupied with a stray dog that had taken refuge in the shadow of our building; who knows how long he had been out there. I spent the next hour coaxing him into the office and giving him water and affection. During that time, the call had come through and Biden was declared the winner. It was hilarious to me that after four years of being glued to the news, not missing a single second, being dialed into every twist and turn, I missed the final call that solidified Biden as the winner. But I didn't need to see it. It was just important that it had happened, and I was clearly where I was supposed to be.

For only the second time in more than 70 years, a Democrat would carry Arizona in a presidential election, a colossal seachange for a state that for generations was considered a bastion of Republican politics. Three key shifts in the state, coupled with messaging to these specific groups, helped Democrats secure a historic victory:

1. A growing Latino population that leans Democratic.

2. A sharp surge in voters moving to Arizona from blue states.

3. An exodus of moderate Republicans and suburban voters from the GOP to the independent or Democratic columns, shepherded by important voices like Cindy McCain.

Misses and Unwarranted Criticism

Biden had secured Arizona 49.4% to 49.1%. Mark Kelly had trounced Senator McSally. Our U.S. House Democrats held their seats. We gained a seat on the vital Corporation Commission. Sheriff Penzone was elected to four more years in the state's most populous county, obliterating Jerry Sheridan in the vote count. Nationally, Democrats maintained control of the U.S. House, albeit by a slimmer margin. And we were within striking distance in the U.S. Senate, with two run-offs in Georgia set to determine the makeup of the Legislative branch.

Where Democrats fell short in Arizona were our down-ballot races, although our losses were far more minimal than the rest of down-ballot Democratic losses across the country, due to our years of organizing, grassroots engagement, and our disciplined communications strategies. These losses in Arizona primarily occurred in state Legislature races in part because of ballot splitting and an unexpected Republican surge in a state with more registered Republicans than Democrats or Independents. We did gain a State Senate seat but came up shortto flip both Houses. We did maintain our number in the House but didn't make gains. The high enthusiasm among both parties had led to two waves crashing into one another, with the Republicans having a slightly bigger splash down-ballot. Conventional wisdom suggests that high turnout favors Democrats. Not when Trumpism is on the ballot. Republicans with Trump at the top of the ticket had an impressive turnout, which blunted the Democratic wave.

But many independents voted for Biden and Kelly, including suburban moms who were turned off by Trump's extremism. Voters may not like divided government, but the splitting of the ticket tells us they either don't recognize ticket-splitting contributes to this, or they consciously want this for "checks and balances." Checks and balances only work when both parties are operating in good faith. When one decides to cow to an authoritarian president, the original theories of the founding fathers go out the window. This issue of ticket splitting requires greater study. But something that solves this, quite simply, is voter registration coupled with mobilization.

While Democrats had done a remarkable job in closing the voter registration gap since 2018, there remains a voter registration deficit with the AZGOP. As I write this, some 35% of Arizona voters are registered with the Republican Party, 32% percent are Democrats, and 31% are not registered with either party. Because of this, Democrats remain reliant on independent and moderate voters. Until that deficit flips, this will be the name of the game for foreseeable cycles. When that registration deficit changes over, it must be by a wide Democratic margin because, sadly, being registered doesn't guarantee that a person will actually exercise their right to vote. Until this happens, Democratic messaging will have to be measured so as not to alienate middle-of-the-road voters.

Because we recognized this fact in 2020, Democrats carried the top of the ticket in Arizona. However, down-ballot Democratic candidates, significantly those in Maricopa County, paid the price because of vote splitting, due in part to higher Republican turnout. As I mentioned, Republicans had more registered voters.

Something that Arizona Democrats were highly successful in, and that ultimately played a key role in our strong mail-in vote performance, was the roughly 75,000 new Permanent Early Voting List subscribers we enrolled for the 2020 election. While Arizona has a long history of voting by mail, in this cycle it proved to be more important than ever before in 2020, and I'm proud that we got so many new voters signed up to send their ballots in through the postal service.

While falling short in various down-ballot races was frustrating and required reflection and recalibration, we had never expected to blow away Republicans in one fell swoop. We always knew Arizona was going to be close. And we did not sustain the losses felt across the country. Immediately, there were critics, armchair generals, and those with agendas who wanted to chalk up the entire election as a failure and point fingers. I understand the disappointment, but I disagree with their assessment. Their argument was essentially the equivalent of getting pissed off at their team for winning Game 7 of the World Series but not pitching a no-hitter. We won the game. And next season we're poised to keep winning.

Could there have been more investment in other places? Of course. Were there things to fix? Yes. Were opportunities missed? Certainly in some cases. We will need to constantly refine our language and make sure we leverage the right messengers. That's more than just ads, it's spokespeople, it's talk shows, it's radio, it's brand ambassadors who can help to illustrate our values organically. Did every candidate up and down the ballot get the attention from the party they deserved? No, of course not. But no one can seriously deny that we achieved a historic victory. Sure, we didn't get everything we wanted, but Arizona is poised to be in the spotlight for years to come, with another Senate race slated for 2022 and another in 2024. And now we have the infrastructure to compete and expand our victory.

Our chair had stated for months that she would not be running for her position again, having served in the voluntary position for nearly four years. But some in the media decided to spin that as a sign that she was somehow leaving as a failure because she hadn't secured the state Legislature. Never mind that Arizona picked up two Democratic senators for the first time in 70 years on her watch. Never mind that Arizona voted for the Democratic presidential candidate for the first time since 1996. Never mind that she helped secure a Democratic secretary of state, helped elect two Democrats to the Corporation Commission, and helped Democrats gain and retain our U.S. House Democratic majority. The viewpoint that our chair was in any way not seeking re-election because she had somehow "failed" was flat out wrong. Chair Rotellini had helped make history and was entitled to a reprieve. Naturally, after every election cycle, fingers point, people make excuses, and blame gets passed around. I can attest that the party did everything in its power to win races across the state, and I recognize there is more work to be done and areas to improve upon, but we had a history-making victory and our chair's contribution to that is indisputable.

With Arizona's flip to blue, the state is following in the footsteps of its neighbors Nevada and Colorado, where Democrats have taken control of many aspects of government and moved their states from a traditional rightward lean. As we had known for quite some time, victory would not have been possible without securing Maricopa County, home to Phoenix and nearly 60% of all people in the state. Biden was just the second Democrat to win Arizona since 1948, when Harry Truman won. Bill Clinton narrowly won the state in 1996 but lost Maricopa County, while his fellow Democrats lost a slew of down-ballot races. Arizona moved farther right in the next two decades, electing immigration hard-liners like Governor Jan Brewer and Maricopa County Sheriff Joe Arpaio. To avoid that, the work must go on.

What Worked and What to Ramp Up

Battleground states emerge and change all of the time. In 2022 I believe they will be Arizona, Georgia, Florida, Michigan, Wisconsin, Pennsylvania, Minnesota, North Carolina, and Ohio. I believe that despite historical precedent, where the party in control of the White House faces midterm backlash, the Senate will be hard to maintain for the GOP. It will be critical for Democratic state parties to win tight races in 2022 and 2024 shortly thereafter.

Our 2020 Democratic victory in Arizona built on the work by grassroots organizations, many of which focused on the state's growing Latino population by uniting around the opposition to the right-wing immigration crackdowns. It is worth noting that these organizations did not have a presence or any semblance of influence in 1996. These groups provided the state's Democratic apparatus in the mid 2010s, electrifying a growing and influential voting bloc that helped secure aDemocratic Senate seat in 2018 and, two years later, another Senate seat as well as the presidential race.

Keeping in mind Florida's demographically heavy Cuban American population, Biden won Arizona with a big majority of Latino voters becauseDemocrats did things they neglected to do in Florida and Texas. Joe Biden went on the airwaves in Arizona at the end of June, spent millions of dollars on bilingual communications, and never backed off, whereas a budget-crunched Trump camp turned their TV ads on and off. When all was said and done, Biden out-advertised Trump in every part of the day, often by a margin of more than three to one.

There were numerous Latinx+Hispanic organizations in Arizona telling Latinos and Hispanics why they should be voting for Biden, and they used various mediums to spread that message. The Mission for Arizona team also trained over 1,600 volunteers in Spanish and those volunteers were able to talk to thousands of Spanish-speaking voters in their preferred language. These were the integral reasons why Arizona had success for Biden whereas Florida and Texas had different results. Additionally, Democrats believe demographics are destiny. That's true and nice if you have 50+ years. But if you have 6 or 18 months, demography is not so much destiny as it is decelerated change. Demographics may ultimately be destiny, but minority voters are not a monolith, and demographics take time to adjust. In 25 years we may truly reap the benefits of shifting demographics, but it's hard to make that dream a reality in two-or four-year cycles. We need to keep our hands on the wheel and foot on the gas when it comes to engaging and mobilizing these communities; otherwise, we will lose in the short term.

We were also obviously successful because of the migration of suburban moms from the Republican Party, as well as moderate Republicans who previously supported leaders like Senator McCain. Arizona's large independent block also broke our way. This also included Mormon voters who traditionally held a conservative disposition but were turned off by Trump and GOP extremism. These results are a testament to our thread-the-needle, universal values driven messaging strategy.

The Defund the Police rhetoric, coupled with some Democrats leaning into the Democratic Socialist label, gave Republicans an opening I think many folks took for granted. While only a small handful of progressive candidates were actually for defunding the police, a majority of House Democrats, along with Joe Biden, rejected that slogan, as did the Arizona Democratic Party and most Democrats. But that wasn't enough to effectively counter attacks. From my perspective, we should have countered the messaging of socialism by labeling Trump and his enablers as fascists, forced them to defend that label, and explained it away just as they were making most Democrats do with socialism. We should have countered the Defund the Police rhetoric by giving more national prominence to elected Democrats in law enforcement, not using them to endorse candidates but to share their perspectives on the benefits of police reform.

The impact of COVID-19 certainly had a role to play among Trump and Biden supporters. Those backing Trump regularly gave him the benefit of the doubt on the virus, arguing that he was being scape-goated, regardless of the president's own admissions of downplaying the virus and slowing testing. For many Biden supporters, the virus was in the front of their minds, and many blamed Trump.

My personal assessment is that the virus served as an additional motivator but was not the key factor that delivered Arizona to Biden. Arguably, our victory could have been greater had we been able to hold in-person events and campaign in a traditional fashion. Tactically, however, we executed the most successful Democratic campaign in recent Arizona history.

Starting early allowed the Mission for Arizona team to develop rela-tionships, train new volunteers, and focus on PEVL. They signed up over 75,000 voters on PEVL and identified voters for Democrats up and down the ballot. COVID-19 presented new problems, but the team was still able to build a colossal digital organizing program to vir-tually train thousands of volunteers on Zoom, send over 12.6 million text messages, and hold digital house parties. The coordinated cam-paign had over 150 members in their organizing staff covering every precinct and over 250 staff statewide. They also built the largest vot-er-protection team in Arizona history and worked with the county partners to build a tribal organizing program that mobilized turnout across the state.

Despite the issues and concerns about 2020 down-ballot losses, I see additional successes on the horizon. We have Democratic infrastructure in Arizona that we didn't have in the late '90s, we now have substantial wins under our belt, and with those comes a new generation of Arizona Democrats who know victory instead of incessant defeat. And finally, we have strong coalitions that can help us continue to advance the ball for years to come. In order to continue to win statewide, Democrats and progressive groups must continue to expand the electorate and attract swing voters.

Un-American Antics

In the weeks that followed the election, Trump and his Republican enablers across the country and, unfortunately, in Arizona, did their best to undermine integrity in the election. They cried fraud with no evidence, filed lawsuits with no basis in reality, and spread false information in an attempt to convince voters that somehow the election had been rigged. This lit a fire under right-wing radicals, who protested outside election offices, made death threats against elected Democrats and our staff, and tried to intimidate our 11 electors.

Their efforts were futile, the majority of Americans recognizing their scheme, but the fact that this even happened is disturbing, and the individuals who took part in this sham represent the absolute worst of our country. On January 6, 2021, this fervor peaked when insurrectionists at Trump's behest stormed the U.S. Capitol during the Electoral College certification. These terrorists desecrated our Capitol, assaulted police, and took lives, but they did not defeat Democracy. Our response to the attack was swift and in the weeks that followed we would be bold in our calls for investigations into Arizona lawmakers presumed to have been involved in perpetrating and supporting the insurrection. I'm hopeful that anyone who had a part in fueling or participating in this treasonous act is brought to justice. While these un-American antics continue through today, with ridiculous ballot audits and attacks on ballot access, I'm confident that Democrats and the American people will persevere through these oppressive actions just as they have always done.

The Triumph

On December 14, Arizona's 11 electors, including our chair, officially voted to send our state's electoral votes to the Biden-Harris ticket. This much was clear: in Arizona and across the country, the righteous might of the vast majority of Americans had won through to absolute victory. The tragedy of 2016 had been remedied; we had adjusted course in the arc of history.

In the months after the election, focus inevitably pivoted to 2022, and the Arizona Democratic Party staff began working toward the next election while ushering in new state party leadership. Something I feel the general public is unaware of is the dedication and tireless work of the Arizona Democratic Party staff. People will never fully know or understand the sacrifice that comes with these jobs, the long hours, the thanklessness, and the ever-present criticism. The unwavering and honorable leadership of Chair Rotellini, Executive Director Herschel Fink, and Chief of Staff Kelly Paisley amidst an unprecedented election year inspired our team and helped us be successful. I can't stress enough that the people who work at all levels of the state party did an amazing job, and their contributions helped to save our Democracy.

In closing, the bottom line is this: just six years ago Arizona was seen as a Republican lock. The questions now are: will the surge in Democratic strength continue, and will it put Arizona further out of reach in the years to come? Our collective efforts in the upcoming cycles will be critical in making that a reality, and leveraging the infrastructure and best practices we have put in place now will be vital. We cannot afford to go backward, to reinvent the wheel as we have so often done in the past. We must seize this moment and capitalize. At the time of this writing, President Biden has a narrow Democratic-controlled House and Senate. Now all eyes turn to 2022 and whether the president can expand his majority and keep America on the right course. The strategies of Democrats in current and future battleground states will be crucial.

Our Statement on November 7, 2020

For Immediate Release

Saturday, November 7, 2020

Contact: Matt Grodsky, mgrodsky@azdem.org

Arizona Democratic Party Statement On A Historic Election

Chair Felecia Rotellini issued the following statement:

"Arizona Democrats have made history. The Grand Canyon State is now blue.

"We now have two Democratic Senators, an achievement we have not seen in over 50 years. And Arizona has delivered its 11 electoral college votes to now President-elect Joe Biden.

"We are a part of the broadest coalition ever assembled by a Democratic presidential nominee in Arizona. From leaders like our Congressional Delegation, our Mayors and our state legislators, to voters from all walks of life and every corner of our state, people of faith and conscience—we've built the kind of team we needed to succeed.

"I want to thank the Arizona Democratic Party staff, Mission

For Arizona and the Arizona Democratic Legislative Campaign Committee for their tireless work and our volunteers and community organizers for their commitment and perseverance in this election and in elections past.

"I want to acknowledge our Democratic Counties and Legislative Districts for their resilience and leadership. Our teams across the state ran an extraordinary early voting program and an unprecedented "get out the vote" effort that led to Arizonans casting more votes in early voting than cast in all of 2016.

"Thank you to all of our candidates, up and down the ballot, for continuing the fight for Arizona families. Your courage and fortitude paved the way for so many victories and this record voter turnout.

"Finally, thank you to the voters of Arizona. These victories truly transcend party politics. Democrats, Republicans, and Independents came together to elect leaders that will put the people first. The future looks bright for our great state and nation."

✦ ✦ ✦

HOW TO USE COMMUNICATIONS
TO WIN BATTLEGROUNDS

E very battleground state is different, but a state becomes a battle-ground when there is a near-even divide between Republicans and Democrats or enough voters up for grabs in the center to tip the scales. This means that the party with the most extreme ideological spectrum typically loses because they alienate the middle.

In the aftermath of the Democratic victories in Georgia and the Capitol insurrection, there were nationwide concerns about the power of the filibuster in a narrowly controlled Democratic Senate. Democrats from sea to shining sea were calling for aggressive action so that Biden's legislative agenda could be successful. I am in complete support of their passion and believe aggressive action should be taken to advance these much needed and popular policies. But great care should be exercised with how we message. The risk posed to Democrats in battleground states is the allure of pivoting too hard to the left too quickly. As good as it might feel to lean into the base, discipline is destiny in battlegrounds.

I am not suggesting that messaging must shy away from core Democratic values, but I am suggesting that it's a matter of tactics. The way you deliver a message about Democratic priorities can make or break your state's chances of going blue or staying locked in an ever-constant battle.

When we began our journey in 2020, we had a choice to make: heed every impulse to amplify our most passionate feelings around key Democratic issues or illustrate our values to the public in a way that would resonate broadly. We chose the latter not only because it was a sound messaging strategy but because at the end of the day most Americans want their representatives to lead for all of them and not just some of them, regardless of party.

Right now, the GOP is in a war with itself and that plays to the advantage of Democratic communications teams in battleground states. In 2021, the Arizona GOP controversially re-elected, albeit narrowly, Kelli Ward as their chair, all but guaranteeing more Trumpist messaging in 2022. In fact, Republicans doubled down on their cannibalism and censured Cindy McCain, former Senator Jeff Flake, and Governor Ducey in the same meeting. I have not elaborated on every post 2020 development but undoubtedly the ongoing Republican fanaticism represents an opening for Democrats in Arizona, who elected a new Chairwoman, State Representative Raquel Terán, in January 2021. Terán is a progressive leader who has a track record of coalition-building. This will be a vital skill for 2022 as Arizona Democrats look to expand their base without alienating persuadable voters they'll need to attract.

The GOP's relentless devotion to extremism isn't limited to Arizona. The New Hampshire Republican Party had a disastrous reorganization meeting in 2021 that played host to more irresponsible rhetoric that fueled insurrectionist behavior. In the wake of Democrats winning the Senate, and the second impeachment trial of Donald Trump, Republican Senator Rob Portman of Ohio announced he would not seek re-election in 2022, opening up an opportunity for Democrats in another battleground state and throwing the pressure on Republicans to run a Trumpian candidate or someone more moderate.

Republican Senator Richard Burr of North Carolina announced he would not run again in 2022, putting that state in play. Republican Senator Pat Toomey announced in October 2020 that he would not seek reelection in 2022, something that promises to thrust Pennsylvania into the spotlight once more. There will surely be more retirements to come. Additionally, Arizona Governor Ducey announced he would not challenge Senator Kelly in 2022, meaning that Republicans will have to decide whether to run an extremist or a moderate to take on Senator Kelly in two short years. It remains to be seen if they will manage to lose three consecutive Senate races in four years. In the run-up to 2022, America will undergo redistricting, with some states poised to lose or gain congressional seats. This will be musical chairs on steroids as elected officials and rising stars jockey for office. This means that battleground states will be all the more important, unpredictable, and likely flush with campaign cash. With 2022 as the new priority and 2024 looming, Democratic communications teams of state and county parties should be looking at these developments now and crafting messaging strategies that motivates their base but also appeals to voters who may not be life-long Democrats but are also unattracted to GOP chaos.

You are a communications professional working at a Democratic State Party in a battleground state. Or perhaps you're on staff at a county party trying to learn how to flip your red state to blue in 2022. Maybe you're thinking about running as a Democrat but want to hone your swing state message. Or maybe you're just a political junkie trying to figure out winning communications strategies. If you are any of those people, remember this lesson: Communications alone do not decide elections. You need a strong ground game, you need good organizers, and you need money. But communications sets a tone that syndicates across an entire party and campaign. Communications can make winning easier or harder; the choice rests with communications professionals and leaders in your organization.

If you need any more convincing about the arguments made in this book, I'll close with this: We sought to flip a battleground state while at a voter registration disadvantage where a Democratic presidential nominee had not won in nearly a quarter-century. The process we followed was designed to build broad appeal and push us over the top. In the days leading up to the election, October 15, 2020, a *New York Times* op-ed by Dr. Samara Klar and Dr. Christopher Weber of the University of Arizona School of Government and Public Policy read in part, "What partisans want is no longer necessarily reflected in what their parties have to offer—Arizonans, often moderate Democrats and Republicans, have been left up for grabs in the middle while major-party candidates have often moved to opposite ends of the ideological spectrum. And that is an overlooked but essential factor to explain our swinging state: The Arizona Democratic Party is more effectively targeting its messages to align with the moderate voters of the state. Demographic trends suggest that Arizona is moving to the left ideologically. But a better explanation might be that the state is moving toward the ideological center—and that's where winning candidates place themselves." Now compare that assessment with Arizona's election results and you can see the validity of their argument.

With that in mind, my fellow battleground Democratic communications professionals, use your newfound messaging might to win your state.

SOURCES

1996 Canvass Arizona Election. (n.d.). Retrieved from https://azsos.gov/sites/default/files/canvass1996ge.pdf

Ahmaud Arbery: Third man charged over death of black jogger. (2020, May 22). Retrieved from https://www.bbc.com/news/world-us-canada-52764898

Asmelash, L. (2020, August 26). Jacob Blake's mom says he'd be upset over the unrest in city where he came for a fresh start. Retrieved from https://www.cnn.com/2020/08/25/us/who-is-jacob-blake-trnd/index.html

Arizona Democratic Party Statement On A Historic Election. (2020, November 07). Retrieved from https://azdem.org/arizona-democratic-party-statement-on-a-historic-election/

Arizona Democratic Party Statement on Impeachment. (2019, September 25). Retrieved from https://azdem.org/impeachment/

Arizona Democratic Party Statement On The Biden-Harris Ticket. (2020, August 11). Retrieved from https://azdem.org/arizona-democratic-party-statement-on-the-biden-harris-ticket/

Arizona Democratic Party Statement: Courage & Conviction. (2020, February 05). Retrieved from https://azdem.org/impeachmentarticles/

Arizona Democratic Party, M. (2020, March 15). MSNBC Coverage ahead of March 17th Election. Retrieved from https://www.facebook.com/AZDemParty/videos/2547212125519678

Arizona Democratic Primary Results. (2020, March 20). Retrieved from https://www.usatoday.com/elections/results/primaries/democratic/arizona/

Arizona Democrats Put Early Organizing Focus on The Navajo Nation. (2020, January 23). Retrieved from https://azdem.org/navajonation/

Arizona Election Results 2016: President Live Map by County, Real-Time Voting Updates. (n.d.). Retrieved from https://www.politico.com/2016-election/results/map/president/arizona/

Arizona Election Results 2018: Live Midterm Map by County & Analysis. (1970, November 07). Retrieved from https://www.politico.com/election-results/2018/arizona/

Arizona: Trade Statistics. (n.d.). Retrieved from https://globaledge.msu.edu/states/arizona/tradestats

Arizona's Top Trading Partners Span Five Continents. (2019, June 12). Retrieved from https://www.azeconomy.org/2019/06/economy/arizonas-top-trading-partners-span-five-continents/

Asian and Pacific Islander American Vote. (n.d.) Retrieved from https://www.apiavote.org/sites/default/files/2020-02/Arizona-2020.pdf

Axelrod, T. (2020, August 08). Joe Arpaio loses bid for his old position as sheriff. Retrieved from https://thehill.com/homenews/campaign/511146-joe-arpaio-loses-bid-for-his-old-position-as-sheriff

AZ Dems Launch "Mission for Arizona" Coordinated Campaign. (2020, February 18). Retrieved from https://mailchi.mp/missionforarizona/m4az-launch?e=025ca9bb20

Bates, J. (2020, January 15). Arizona Rep. Kirkpatrick to Get Treatment for 'Alcohol Dependence'. Retrieved from https://time.com/5765930/arizona-rep-ann-kirkpatrick-alcohol-dependence/

Black Lives Matter. (n.d.) Retrieved from https://azdem.org/blacklivesmatter/

Budryk, Z. (2019, September 25). Cindy McCain: I can see Arizona 'going Democrat' in 2020. Retrieved from https://thehill.com/homenews/campaign/463023-cindy-mccain-i-can-see-arizona-going-democrat-in-2020

Carrega, C., & Ghebremedhin, S. (2020, November 17). Timeline: Inside the investigation of Breonna Taylor's killing and its aftermath. Retrieved from https://abcnews.go.com/us/timeline-inside-investigation-breonna-taylors-killing-aftermath/story?id=71217247

Cava, M. (2020, August 10). Activists working in John Lewis' shadow warn about voter suppression ahead of November vote. Retrieved from https://www.usatoday.com/story/news/nation/2020/07/25/john-lewis-voting-rights-act-lawmakers-activists-honor-fallen-leader/5475879002/

CBS News. (2018, November 13). Progressive Dems back off "Abolish ICE" at first meeting since midterms. Retrieved from https://www.cbsnews.com/news/progressive-dems-back-off-abolish-ice-at-first-meeting-since-midterms/

Chan, M. (2018, December 06). Franklin Roosevelt Infamy Speech: Pearl Harbor Transcript. Retrieved from https://time.com/4593483/pearl-harbor-franklin-roosevelt-infamy-speech-attack/

Cillizza, C. (2021, January 25). Analysis: Senate Republicans just took 2 big hits to their 2022 chances. Retrieved from https://www.cnn.com/2021/01/25/politics/doug-ducey-rob-portman-2022/index.html

Cleve Wootson, M. (2020, May 09). It took 74 days for suspects to be charged in the death of a black jogger. Many people are asking why it took so long. Retrieved from https://www.washingtonpost.com/national/outraged-by-the-delayed-arrests-in-killing-of-black-jogger-protesters-in-georgia-demand-justice/2020/05/08/8e7d212a-90a9-11ea-9e23-6914ee410a5f_story.html

Cohen, D. (2020, August 16). Poll: Harris viewed more favorably than unfavorably. Retrieved from https://www.politico.com/news/2020/08/16/kamala-harris-polling-veep-396100

Cooper, J. (2020, November 04). Biden wins Arizona, flips longtime Republican stronghold. Retrieved from https://apnews.com/article/election-2020-joe-biden-donald-trump-race-and-ethnicity-legislature-218ad4d596e87c-6b1a223f19f817776e

Corasaniti, N., & Saul, S. (2020, March 16). Ohio's Governor Postpones Primary as Health Emergency Is Declared Over Virus. Retrieved from https://www.nytimes.com/2020/03/16/us/politics/virus-primry-2020-ohio.html

DiStaso, J. (2021, January 24). After 4-hour Zoom chaos, NHGOP adjourns annual meeting with no votes on chair, vice chair. Retrieved from https://www.wmur.com/article/after-4-hour-of-zoom-chaos-nhgop-abruptly-adjourns-annual-meeting-with-no-vote-on-chair-vice-chair/35298030

DuVal, F. (2019, July 31). Choose wisely, Democrats. If we lose Arizona, we could lose the White House. Retrieved from https://www.azcentral.com/story/opinion/op-ed/2019/07/31/democratic-presidential-candidates-need-arizona-win-white-house/1862943001/

Enten, H. (2020, August 16). The Kamala Harris pick is a hit with voters so far. Retrieved from https://www.cnn.com/2020/08/16/politics/kamala-harris-polls-voters-like-pick/index.html

Faller, M. (2020, January 30). New analysis of firearm deaths by ASU finds most victims are suicides. Retrieved from https://asunow.asu.edu/20200130-arizona-impact-new-analysis-firearm-deaths-asu-finds-most-victims-are-suicides

Fatal Force: Police shootings database. (2020, January 22). Retrieved from https://www.washingtonpost.com/graphics/investigations/police-shootings-database/

Fink, E. (2019, September 19). Some Arizona Democratic Party members say Sinema is not progressive enough. Retrieved December 27, 2020, from https://kvoa.com/uncategorized/2019/09/18/some-arizona-democratic-party-members-say-sinema-is-not-progressive-enough/

Following is the transcript of President Bush's speech at Friday's national prayer service, attended by a number of former presidents and many members of Congress, to honor the victims of the terrorist attacks. Retrieved from https://www.washingtonpost.com/wp-srv/nation/specials/attacked/transcripts/bushtext_091401.html

For some young adults, the 2016 US election was a 'traumatic experience'. (2018, October 22). Retrieved from https://www.sciencedaily.com/releases/2018/10/181022150951.htm

Franklin D. Roosevelt – Flag Day Address. (2020, June 14). Retrieved from https://commandperformanceleadership.wordpress.com/2012/06/14/franklin-d-roosevelt-flag-day-address/

Golshan, T. (2016, November 09). Hillary Clinton's concession speech full transcript: 2016 presidential election. Retrieved from https://www.vox.com/2016/11/9/13570328/hillary-clinton-concession-speech-full-trascript-2016-presidential-election

Greenwood, M. (2021, January 01). Seven Senate races to watch in 2022. Retrieved from https://thehill.com/homenews/campaign/530880-seven-senate-races-to-watch-in-2022?rl=1

Gun Safety • Mark Kelly for Senate. Retrieved from https://markkelly.com/issue/gun-safety/

Hamid, S. (2019, December 16). Impeachment Could End Badly. Retrieved from https://www.theatlantic.com/ideas/archive/2019/12/impeachment-warranted-also-bad-idea/603616/

Hansen, R. (2018, July 19). Rep. Kyrsten Sinema sides with House Republicans to support embattled ICE agency. Retrieved from https://www.azcentral.com/story/news/politics/arizona/2018/07/18/kyrsten-sinema-sides-house-republicans-support-embattled-ice/798626002/

Hansen, R. (2020, August 12). Will Biden's veep pick of Kamala Harris boost his campaign in Arizona? Retrieved from https://www.azcentral.com/story/news/politics/arizona/2020/08/11/bidens-veep-pick-kamala-harris-boost-his-campaign-arizona/3348978001/

Hansen, R. J. (2019, October 29). Arizona Democratic chair criticized for saying Trump has 'aligned himself with ISIS'. Retrieved from https://www.azcentral.com/story/news/politics/arizona/2019/10/29/democratic-chair-felecia-rotellini-hit-saying-trump-aligned-isis/2502702001/

Isidore, C. (2020, February 07). How Trump's three years of job gains compares to Obama's. Retrieved from https://www.cnn.com/2020/02/06/economy/trump-obama-jobs-comparison/index.html

Issenberg, S. (2012, September 03). Word Lab: "Bracketing". Retrieved from https://slate.com/news-and-politics/2012/09/bracketing-why-do-political-operatives-use-the-term-to-describe-everything-they-do.html

Jackson, J. (2020, May 10). Justice delayed is justice denied. Was Ahmaud Arbery killed for 'jogging while black'? Retrieved from https://www.cnn.com/2020/05/10/opinions/justice-failed-ahmaud-arbery-jackson/index.html

Jamal Khashoggi: All you need to know about Saudi Journalist's Death. (2021, February 24). Retrieved from https://www.bbc.com/news/world-europe-45812399

Janowski, E. (2020, February 05). Timeline: Trump impeachment inquiry. Retrieved January 03, 2021, from https://www.nbcnews.com/politics/trump-impeachment-inquiry/timeline-trump-impeachment-inquiry-n1066691

Jeon, H. (2020, July 22). What "Defund the Police" Means - and Why Some Activists Say Reform Is Not Enough. Retrieved from https://www.good-housekeeping.com/life/a33024951/defund-the-police-meaning/

Jeremy Duda, A. (2020, September 22). Arizona sees "historic HIGH" turnout for primary election • Arizona Mirror. Retrieved from https://www.azmirror.com/blog/arizona-sees-historic-high-turnout-for-primary-election/

Jeremy Duda, A. (2019, December 16). Poll shows support for impeaching Trump, but not removing him from office ◆ Arizona Mirror. Retrieved from https://www.azmirror.com/blog/poll-shows-support-for-impeaching-trump-but-not-removing-him-from-office/

Kimbel-Sannit, A. (2019, December 17). Democratic fundraising titans prepare for Arizona clash in 2020. Retrieved from https://azcapitoltimes.com/news/2019/12/13/democratic-fundraising-titans-prepare-for-arizona-clash-in-2020/

Klar, S., & Weber, C. (2020, October 15). Why Would a Republican Vote Biden? Ask Arizonans. Retrieved from https://www.nytimes.com/2020/10/15/opinion/arizona-biden-trump-2020.html

Luhby, T. (2020, January 11). Many millennials are worse off than their parents—a first in American history. Retrieved from https://www.cnn.com/2020/01/11/politics/millennials-income-stalled-upward-mobility-us/index.html

MacKinley Lutes-Adlhoch and Christopher Scragg/Cronkite News. (2020, February 10). Arizonans among surprise Trump guests for state of the Union address. Retrieved from https://cronkitenews.azpbs.org/2020/02/05/arizonans-among-surprise-trump-guests-for-state-of-the-union-address/

Maricopa County Attorney Allister Adel talks about Dion Johnson case. (2020, September 22). Retrieved from https://www.azfamily.com/video/maricopa-county-attorney-allister-adel-talks-about-dion-johnson-case/video_1e8809a2-513c-5e8e-9655-9aeb9fe3523a.html

Mike Noble, O. (2019, December 21). Independents and impeachment could determine Arizona's electoral future. Retrieved from https://thehill.com/opinion/campaign/475588-independents-and-impeachment-could-determine-arizonas-electoral-future

Mind-boggled by Arizona Demographics? Retrieved from https://www.arizona-demographics.com/

News, 1. (2019, December 20). 'SHAME!' painted on Arizona Democratic Party headquarters. Retrieved from https://www.13newsnow.com/article/news/politics/shame-painted-on-arizona-democratic-party-headquarters/75-6dfc39c6-3b07-4dfc-96e9-ebc5ab01a977

News, I. (2019, November 05). With the election a year off, Arizona could become a key player. Retrieved from https://cronkitenews.azpbs.org/2019/11/05/arizona-2020-primary-election-role/

News, M. (2019, November 08). State GOP looks to clear nomination path for Trump by canceling primary. Retrieved from https://cronkitenews.azpbs.org/2019/09/06/state-gop-looks-to-clear-nomination-path-for-trump-by-canceling-primary/

Passwaiter, S. (2020, November 23). Political ad spending this year reached a whopping $8.5 billion. Retrieved from https://adage.com/article/campaign-trail/political-ad-spending-year-reached-whopping-85-bilion/2295646

Philip, A. (2018, November 16). Congratulations, Arizona! Turnout in the 2018 midterms smashed records. Retrieved from https://www.azcentral.com/story/news/politics/elections/2018/11/16/arizona-midterm-voter-turnout-hit-record-propelled-women-young-voters/1994334002/

Politico. (2020, December 16). Women Rule on Apple Podcasts. Retrieved December 27, 2020, from https://podcasts.apple.com/us/podcast/women-rule/id1210928141

POLL: To Impeach or Not to Impeach. (2019, November 14). Retrieved from https://ohpredictive.com/press-releases/trump_impeachment/

Public Broadcasting Service.. *One Beakful At A Time | To The Contrary.* PBS. https://www.pbs.org/to-the-contrary/blog/6996/one-beakful-at-a-time.

Rep. James Clyburn (D-SC) is Interviewed about the Harris Pick; Big 10 and PAC-12 Won't Play this Fall; New Covid-19 Reporting System; Failed Stimulus Talks; Inflation Data Beats Expectations. Aired 9:30- 0a. (2020). Retrieved from http://transcripts.cnn.com/TRANSCRIPTS/2008/12/cnr.02.html

Ruelas, R. (2018, July 12). Arizona Gov. Doug Ducey campaign paints Democrat David Garcia as supporter of #AbolishICE. Retrieved from https://www.azcentral.com/story/news/politics/elections/2018/07/11/david-garcia-call-replace-ice-criticized-arizona-gov-ducey-abolish-ice/777519002/

Sanchez, Y. (2019, September 17). Arizona progressives seek to censure Democratic Sen. Kyrsten Sinema. Retrieved from https://www.azcentral.com/story/news/politics/arizona/2019/09/17/arizona-progressives-seek-censure-democratic-sen-kyrsten-sinema/2356605001/

Shapiro, D. (2020, July 25). Arson suspected in Maricopa County Democratic Party headquarters fire. Retrieved from https://ktar.com/story/3427117/arson-suspected-in-maricopa-county-democratic-party-headquarters-fire/

Silver, N. (2020, December 22). Tracking Congress In The Age Of Trump. Retrieved from https://projects.fivethirtyeight.com/congress-trump-score/kyrsten-sinema/

Stracqualursi, V. (2020, April 28). Arizona GOP chair encourages anti-stay-at-home protesters to dress like health care workers. Retrieved from https://www.cnn.com/2020/04/28/politics/arizona-kelli-ward-coronavirus-protests/index.html

Stratford, M. (2020, November 04). Fox News defends calling Arizona for Biden after pushback from Trump team. Retrieved from https://www.politico.com/news/2020/11/04/fox-news-arizona-election-2020-433997

Taylor, R. (2020, March 18). Joe Biden Speech Transcript on Primary Night: Coronavirus, Economy, Primaries. Retrieved December 28, 2020, from https://www.rev.com/blog/transcripts/joe-biden-speech-transcript-on-primary-night-coronavirus-economy-primaries

Tin, A. (2020, July 29). Ex-volunteer set fire to Arizona county Democrats' office "in retaliation," police say. Retrieved from https://www.cbsnews.com/news/maricopa-county-democrats-office-fire-suspect-charged-with-arson-in-arizona/

Today Show. (2017, June 30). A marriage 20 years in the making—preschool sweethearts finally wed. Retrieved from https://www.today.com/news/20-years-later-these-preschool-sweethearts-got-married-t113358

Voter Registration & Historical Election Data. (n.d.). Retrieved from https://azsos.gov/elections/voter-registration-historical-election-data

Will, G. (2020, March 26). Opinion | A loose brick in Republicans' red wall. Retrieved from https://www.washingtonpost.com/opinions/a-loose-brick-in-republicans-red-wall/2020/03/24/349ce6f0-6dee-11ea-aa80-c2470c6b2034_story.html

Wright, R. (2019, October 21). Turkey, Syria, the Kurds, and Trump's abandonment of foreign policy. Retrieved from https://www.newyorker.com/magazine/2019/10/28turkey-syria-the-kurds-and-trumps-abandonment-of-foreign-policy

2018 Midterms: Exit polling. Retrieved from https://www.cnn.com/election/2018/exit-polls/arizona/senate

ABOUT THE AUTHOR

M Matt Grodsky is the vice president, director of public affairs at Matters of State Strategies. He served as the director of communications for the Arizona Democratic Party from 2019 to 2021 and helped flip the state blue for the first time in nearly a quarter-century. He is an elected precinct committeeman in Arizona and an Arizona Democratic Party state committee member. Matt has managed marketing and communications for dozens of public and private sector clients, and is the winner of over 35 awards for creative work. He is a frequent subject of human interest stories in major media outlets with his wife, Laura.

Follow on Twitter @mattgrodsky

www.ingramcontent.com/pod-product-compliance
Lightning Source LLC
Chambersburg PA
CBHW041258040426
42334CB00028BA/3067